What You Need to Know about Privacy Law

What You Need to Know about Privacy Law

A Guide for Librarians and Educators

GRETCHEN MCCORD

 LIBRARIES UNLIMITED

AN IMPRINT OF ABC-CLIO, LLC
Santa Barbara, California • Denver, Colorado • Oxford, England

Library of Congress Cataloging-in-Publication Data

McCord, Gretchen.
    What you need to know about privacy law : a guide for librarians and educators / Gretchen McCord.
        pages cm
    Includes bibliographical references and index.
    ISBN 978–1–61069–081–2 (hardcopy : alk. paper) — ISBN 978–1–61069–082–9 (ebook) 1. Privacy, Right of—United States. 2. Student records—Law and legislation—United States. 3. Data protection—Law and legislation—United States. I. Title.
KF1263.E38M33   2013
342.7308′5802437—dc23   2013015217

ISBN: 978–1–61069–081–2
EISBN: 978–1–61069–082–9

17 16 15 14 13   1 2 3 4 5

This book is also available on the World Wide Web as an eBook.
Visit www.abc-clio.com for details.

Libraries Unlimited
An Imprint of ABC-CLIO, LLC

ABC-CLIO, LLC
130 Cremona Drive, P.O. Box 1911
Santa Barbara, California 93116-1911

This book is printed on acid-free paper (∞)

Manufactured in the United States of America

To Joe, Myrtis, and Dominick, from the bottom of my heart

Contents

Preface

Privacy law is a very complicated area of law, for many reasons. To start with: What do we mean when we use the word "privacy"? What types of information do we believe should be respected as private? To what extent should the law answer these questions? Should we rely on legislation to protect our privacy, or voluntary industry self-regulation, or a combination of both? The only two answers on which we constantly find agreement are "It depends" and "The answers constantly change over time." Our concepts as a society about privacy—what should remain private and who should enforce our right to that privacy—change as our society changes. What our grandparents considered to be purely private matters, we discuss openly with our friends or colleagues. Undoubtedly, topics we choose not to share around the water fountain today will soon be topics for open discussion amongst our grandchildren, if not already.

In the current technological environment, when we so easily share sometimes intimate details of our personal lives with scores of "friends" on social media sites, and when it is increasingly easy to find all sorts of information about individuals online, is an expectation of privacy practical or even possible? Mark Zuckerberg, the young and exuberant founder of Facebook, is infamous for his repeated statements suggesting his disregard for the privacy of Facebook users. (See, e.g., Kirkpatrick 2010; Van Buskirk 2010.) But even as far back as 1999, preceding the birth of Facebook by five years and even the launch of Google, the CEO of Sun Microsystems blatantly eschewed the idea that we have any right to privacy, saying, "You have zero privacy anyway. Get over it." (Sprenger 1999). But how do we—across generations, education levels, economic levels, and subcultures—actually feel about privacy, and what do we expect and even demand?

Studies show that we still believe in, want, and even demand privacy. According to a 2010 national survey, 87 percent of adults are concerned with the security of their personal information on the Internet; 88 percent believe that tracking the sites to which an Internet user goes without their permission is an unfair business practice; and 91 percent believe that it is an unfair business practice for a company to relax its privacy policy after it has already collected personal information (Zogby International 2010, 1). Further, a significant number of adults believe that government should have a major role in enforcing online privacy. The same study found that 49 percent of adults believe the government should play a greater role in regulating the protection of online consumer privacy, while only 36 percent do not; 88 percent believe that legal protections for online privacy should be similar to those offline; 79 percent would support a national "do not track list" similar to the "do not call list"; and 79 percent believe that law enforcement should be required to obtain a warrant to be able to track where a user goes online, while only 12 percent believe they should not (*Id.*). A 2012 survey polling nationwide opinions about targeted advertising online found that 73 percent of adults would object to a search engine tracking searches and using the information to personalize results for future searches because doing so constitutes an invasion of privacy (*Id.* at 2).

Conventional wisdom tells us that members of the younger generation, growing up in the midst of the explosion of social media, who have never not known the Internet, have no qualms about revealing very personal information to strangers—basically, that they have no expectation of, or, more importantly, concern about, privacy.

Contrary to this conventional wisdom, however, studies clearly show that younger generations have very similar expectations of and concerns about privacy as do older. A 2010 survey by the Pew Internet & American Life Project compared the attitudes regarding privacy of adults aged 18 to 24 with those of older cohorts and found that they are not statistically different on any of the topics on which the study polled, with the exception of checking credit reports (Hoofnagle et al. 2010 at 10). The reason for the popular belief that young adults are not as concerned about their privacy, the study concluded, arises from their misperceptions of how well their privacy is actually protected, combined with that age group's propensity towards more risky behavior and decision-making generally (*Id.* at 4–5).

A 2007 Pew study of the behavior of teenagers using social networking suggests that more teenagers are concerned about online privacy than one might expect, and they engage in a variety of techniques to disguise their personal details on social networking sites. The study found that 55 percent of teenagers who use the Internet had online profiles; doubtless, the number has increased since the study was conducted. Of those, 66 percent limit access to those profiles in some way. Of those who do not limit access to their profiles, 46 percent say they provide at least some false information on their profiles, sometimes for the purpose of protecting themselves. While 26 percent of teens provide their complete names in online profiles, only 11 percent of those do not limit access to their profiles (Lenhart and Madden 2007, ii, 17).

Clearly, Americans of all ages believe that their privacy should be protected. Many believe that the law provides much greater protection than it actually does. And yet, the very types of information that most Americans believe should remain private, as shown in these studies, have tremendous value in our national economy. The data mining industry earns hundreds of millions, if not billions, of dollars every year by mining and selling that information (Singer 2012). Internet giants like Google and Facebook make most of their profits from targeted advertising built on the data they collect from their consumers (Sasso 2012). Furthermore, new business models continue to develop around the concept of data mining and targeted advertising. (See, e.g., Vega 2012.) Even the federal government purchases databases of personal information from commercial data-mining companies (Solove and Schwartz 2011, 359).

How do we write and interpret law to address privacy in the age of such strongly conflicting ideas about the value of privacy versus the value of data? Some jurisdictions create laws broadly addressing the protection of certain types of information about individuals, regardless of the context in which it is used, such as the European Union's Data Protection Directive. (See European Commission 2012.) The United States has no single, blanket law addressing privacy; rather, U.S. laws address the protection of certain types of information in specific contexts or situations. Instead of taking a holistic approach, both federal and state governments in the United States seem to write legislation in response to constituents' demands, as issues arise. For example, as Internet usage exploded, so did public concern for the safety of children online; in response, Congress passed the Children's Online Privacy Protection Act, providing regulations to protect the privacy of personal data about children. Similarly, as Americans reeled from the shock of the September 11 attacks and the feelings of extreme vulnerability they revealed, Congress passed the USA PATRIOT Act, which diminished well-established protections for citizens' privacy, in an attempt to provide the government with more tools to protect national security.

Because federal statutory law on privacy in the United States is silent on many important areas, state laws have stepped in. That means that the protection of certain types of information about you may differ from state to state, such as an employer's ability to require employees or potential employees to provide them with passwords to the employee's social media accounts. Likewise, your responsibilities to protect the privacy of others, and restrictions on your ability to collect and use information about others, may vary from state to state.

Furthermore, this patchwork approach to making law regularly results in unequivocal contradiction between the laws of different jurisdictions. The law of one state may directly contravene the law of another; and a federal court in one jurisdiction sometimes interprets federal law in a significantly different manner than the court in another jurisdiction. As a result, the citizens of one state may, in any given context, have not only entirely different rights and responsibilities, but opposing rights and responsibilities, than those of another state.

While new privacy laws are being passed at both state and local levels, the continuing development of technology muddles up everything. We know that technology changes at the pace of a rocket, while changes in law crawl along at the pace of a snail. So what happens when advances in technology create new issues for privacy protection? Often, the courts must fill the gaps in our laws by interpreting existing statutory law to apply to a new situation for which it was not written.

By now, you probably have a clear appreciation for how complicated privacy law is. Furthermore, the laws constantly change, as lawmakers try to respond to changes in society and technology. For that reason, it is impossible to write a book that will accurately address in detail every situation educators may face in this arena. My goal in writing this book is to teach you enough about the law to allow you to feel comfortable facing privacy issues; spot red flags when they arise; generally know what rights you and your students have, and what responsibilities you and your institution have; and give you the tools to confidently move forward, even if you do not immediately know *the* answer to a problem when it arises.

ABOUT THIS BOOK

Audience and Approach

This book is intended to be a guide for those involved in all levels of education: K–12 and postsecondary; public and private; classroom instructors, librarians, administrators, board members, and other professionals in supporting positions. My goal is for readers to come away with an understanding of the overall concepts underlying privacy law in the United States and how it is applied in the educational setting, and how courts analyze the law in that context, so that you will be better prepared to analyze issues as they arise and address them appropriately.

This book is intended to be a user-friendly guide, almost a handbook, to the most pertinent privacy issues faced by those working in this environment. I hope that it will both provide enough background and explanation for readers to understand how the law works, and also serve as a quick reference for addressing privacy issues in specific situations. With that goal in mind, I have forgone significant discussion about the legislative history of statutes mentioned, historical case law, and the social philosophy behind the development of our current law.

That being said, I have tried to emphasize the legislative intent of statutory law and the rationale of the courts in their analyses, with the hope that the reader will learn how to analyze situations he or she faces and respond accordingly.

However, this book is not a replacement for legal advice. When you find yourself in a situation in which you need legal guidance, you should consult your institution's legal department or counsel. Only your institution's legal counsel can provide you with legal advice and guidance. Nothing in this book should be considered or relied upon as legal advice.

Structure

The first section of this book will provide an overview of the current (as of this writing) state of privacy laws in the United States that are most pertinent for educators. The second section will address several broad areas traditionally of concern in the education environment, regardless of technology, and will show how courts have applied the law in such situations. The third section addresses the future of privacy law and provides guidance for how to protect the rights of both educational institutions and their students in the face of a dearth of legal protection. The final section provides a variety of resources for your use as you travel down this winding and constantly changing road.

Terminology

All areas of law use terms of art, and law often applies very specific definitions to what we would otherwise think of as everyday words. To complicate things more, a particular term may mean one thing in one area of law and something different in another area of law. I have tried as much as possible to stay away from using terms of art and legal jargon unless noted otherwise. Thus, no significance should be attached to the use of one word over another unless stated. For example, in discussing constitutional rights under the Fourth Amendment, I interchangeably use the words "infringement" and "violation"; there is no significance to the use of one rather than the other. In the same section, however, the term "reasonableness" does have a specific meaning and relevance, and so I have explained that.

Accuracy of Information Provided in This Book

I have made every effort to ensure that the information provided in this book was timely and accurate at the time it was written, in late 2012. However, new law can be made any day. As I write, Congress is considering both new legislation and major amendments to existing legislation addressing privacy rights in the online context. As you are about to learn, the area of privacy law actually constitutes a collection of many specific pieces of legislation, at both federal and state levels, as well as case law interpreting those statutes. The more statutes that are out there, the more potential exists for some piece of legislation to be amended. This is particularly true in the context of privacy issues in the digital environment, where we constantly encounter new situations to which current law simply does not apply or is insufficient. A growing demand for legislative solutions is pushing both Congress and state legislators to draft new law to address the privacy needs of individuals as well as the information industry (although these laws often contradict each other). Court cases are handed down daily and may interpret or apply existing law in a new or different way. With law being made daily by both legislative bodies and courts at both state and federal levels, it simply is not possible to encapsulate all law related to privacy in one place, short of a full-fledged legal treatise.

For all of these reasons, be aware that it is your responsibility to confirm the current status of any given law before relying on it. Particularly in situations in which your institution is creating policy or making significant decisions with any kind of legal ramifications, you should consult your institution's legal counsel before taking action.

BIBLIOGRAPHY

European Commission, "Protection of Personal Data," http://ec.europa.eu/justice/data-protection/index_en.htm (cited November 12, 2012).

Hoofnagle, Chris, Jennifer King, Su Li, and Joseph Turow, "How Different Are Young Adults from Older Adults When It Comes to Information Privacy Attitudes & Policies?" http://papers.ssrn.com/sol3/papers.cfm?abstract_id=1589864 (April 14, 2010).

Kirkpatrick, Marshall, "Facebook's Zuckerberg Says the Age of Privacy Is Over," http://readwrite.com/2010/01/09/facebooks_zuckerberg_says_the_age_of_privacy_is_ov (January 9, 2010).

Lenhart, Amanda, and Marry Madden, "Teens, Privacy, and Online Social Networks," http://www.pewinternet.org/~/media//Files/Reports/2007/PIP_Teens_Privacy_SNS_Report_Final.pdf.pdf (April 18, 2007).

Purcell, Kristen, Joanna Brenner, and Lee Rainie, "Search Engine Use 2012," http://pewinternet.org/~/media//Files/Reports/2012/PIP_Search_Engine_Use_2012.pdf (March 9, 2012).

Sasso, Brendan, "FTC to Set Framework for Privacy," *The Hill* (March 26, 2012).

Singer, Natasha, "Mapping, and Sharing, the Consumer Genome," http://www.nytimes.com/2012/06/17/technology/acxiom-the-quiet-giant-of-consumer-database-marketing.html?pagewanted=all (June 16, 2012).

Solove, Daniel J., and Paul M. Schwartz, *Privacy, Information, and Technology* (New York: Wolters Kluwer Law & Business, 2011).

Sprenger, Polly, "Sun on Privacy: 'Get Over It'," http://www.wired.com/politics/law/news/1999/01/17538 (January 26, 1999).

Van Buskirk, Eliot, "Report: Facebook CEO Mark Zuckerberg Doesn't Believe in Privacy," http://www.wired.com/business/2010/04/report-facebook-ceo-mark-zuckerberg-doesnt-believe-in-privacy (April 28, 2010).

Vega, Tanzina, "The New Algorithm of Web Marketing," http://www.nytimes.com/2012/11/16/business/media/automated-bidding-systems-test-old-ways-of-selling-ads.html?ref=todayspaper (November 15, 2012).

Zogby International, "Results from June 4–7 Nationwide Poll," http://www.precursorblog.com/files/pdf/topline-report-key-findings.pdf (June 2010).

Acknowledgments

I must acknowledge the contributions of many people to the writing of this book. I thank the many instructors, librarians, students, and attorneys whose dedication inspires me, and whose questions and discussions have led me to continually expand my knowledge in the area of privacy law and my appreciation of the everyday issues they face. I thank the privacy attorneys who have mentored me as I developed my expertise in the field of privacy law. I thank the many individuals and organizations daily fighting the good fight to protect the privacy rights of Americans (and others) who don't even realize how nonexistent or threatened their rights may be.

I especially thank Sharon Coatney, of ABC-CLIO, for her patience and assistance; Myrtis McCord for her time, editing skills, and general mentoring of my writing over many decades; and Dominick DeFlorio for his time and skills in editing my work, for his inspiration, and most of all, for his unblinking, unquestioning, and absolute support of all my choices and adventures.

PART I

STATE OF THE LAW

STRUCTURE OF THE U.S. LEGAL SYSTEM

In the U.S. legal system, the two primary categories of law are statutory law and case law (also called "common law"). "Statutory law" refers to the legislation (codified as "statutes" or "codes") written by Congress and state legislatures. "Case law" refers to the decisions of the courts that interpret those statutes. This book also discusses rights granted by the U.S. Constitution, and the term "constitutional law" is commonly used in legal discussions. However, the Constitution itself does not technically create law. Rather, it grants Congress the right to create certain types of law, and it—primarily through its amendments—guarantees certain rights to the citizenry.

Congress cannot enact laws in areas in which the Constitution does not give it the right to do so, but states can. States can also create legislation addressing the same areas as federal legislation; however, where federal and state law conflict, federal law trumps, or "preempts," state law. Conflict exists when it is impossible to comply with both laws, or when the state law constitutes an obstacle to "the accomplishment and execution of the full purposes and objectives of" the federal law (*Crosby v. National Foreign Trade Council*, 530 U.S. 363, 372–73 (2000)). States may not limit rights granted under federal law, nor may state law allow an act prohibited under federal law. Although these rules sound simple, the application can get complex and complicated.

In the context of civil (noncriminal) law, courts interpret and apply the laws. We have one federal court system, and each state has its own court system. As a general statement, federal courts interpret federal law, and state courts interpret state law, though in reality both courts often hear both types of law. All court systems are established in a layered appellate process, to give the losing party a second chance if it feels the law has not been accurately applied the first time around. The overall structure of state court systems is similar to that of the federal system, although they differ in detail. States use different titles for their courts (for example, the New York "Supreme Court" is on the lowest tier of courts in that state, as opposed to the federal Supreme Court being the highest court in the land), which can become confusing.

The lowest level of the federal court system is the district court. If the losing party at trial in district court thinks that the law has been wrongfully applied or that other mistakes were made during the trial, he or she may appeal his or her case. A losing party cannot appeal just because he or she is unhappy to have lost and wants a second opinion. The appeal will be heard by a court of appeal. The country is divided into 13 regions, or "circuits," each with its own court of appeal. For example, "Ninth Circuit Court" refers to the appellate court serving the western region of the United States.

If the loser at the appellate level wishes to appeal, he or she may petition the U.S. Supreme Court to hear his or her case. The loser in the decision from the highest state courts may also petition the U.S. Supreme Court. The Supreme Court has discretion in choosing its cases. It often chooses to hear cases where the law conflicts in different areas of the country, such as when the Ninth Circuit has interpreted a federal law in a way that conflicts with the Fifth Circuit's interpretation; or in a case whose decision would have significant impact across the country.

Precedent, or "stare decisis," is set within each court system, meaning the courts within that system must abide by the holdings of the higher courts in that system. Second Circuit opinions create precedent for all of the lower courts within that jurisdiction, but they are not precedent for courts within, for example, the Third Circuit. Decisions from other circuits may influence the court, however. Because the Supreme Court is the highest court, its rulings set precedent for all others. Only federal legislation may overrule Supreme Court law.

A NOTE ON APPLICATION OF THE LAW

When a court hears a case, it must apply the relevant law only to the case before it. In other words, it can only consider the facts before it. This can be one of the greatest challenges of our court system: The court must apply the law as it has been decided in prior cases, but the facts differ in each case. Thus, the court must decide if the differences are significant. This is an example of why knowing the rationale used by courts is so important; when we know the rationale behind a court's decision, we can apply that rationale to a different set of facts to come to a decision that is consistent with the prior interpretation of the law.

Nonetheless, due to the great weight given to precedent, facing greatly differing factual situations often creates the greatest areas of conflict in our courts. This comes into play most frequently in cases involving new technology, or the results of new technology. For example, as discussed in Chapters 5 and 6, the current standard for school searches of student belongings was developed long before the omnipresence of cell phones. No clear law has emerged on searching cell phones, but some courts, and a growing number of experts and advocates, have argued that a cell phone is significantly different from a book bag or locker, in that it contains such a large amount of personal information about the student as well others. As of this writing, it seems likely that Congress will pass law addressing this issue in the criminal context, which should influence future holdings in the educational context. Currently, however, it is not clear how courts will address the issues created by this new technology. Institutional policies are particularly valuable in facing situations in which the law is not clear; Chapter 8 discusses writing and implementing privacy policies.

BIBLIOGRAPHY

Crosby v. National Foreign Trade Council, 530 U.S. 363, 372–73 (2000).

CHAPTER 1

The Concept and Origins of Privacy Protection in the United States

WHY DO WE CARE?

The Supreme Court itself has recognized that one duty of our public schools is to teach our young people to become responsible citizens, and the Court has weighed this duty in several of its decisions. (See, e.g., *Shelton v. Tucker*, 364 U.S. 479, 487 (1960); *West Virginia State Bd. of Ed. v. Barnette*, 319 U.S. 624, 637 (1943).) This value forms the foundation for significant portions of the codes of ethics of the major national professional associations for educators and librarians: the National Education Association (NEA), the Association of American Educators (AAE), the American Association of University Professors (AAUP), and the American Library Association (ALA). Furthermore, three of these associations specifically recognize a right to privacy for students. Principle I, Section 8 of the NEA Code of Ethics states that an educator "Shall not disclose information about students obtained in the course of professional service unless disclosure serves a compelling professional purpose or is required by law" (National Education Association 1975). A Joint Statement on Rights and Freedoms of Students issued by the AAUP, the U.S. National Student Association, the Association of American Colleges, and others states: "Information about student views, beliefs, and political associations that professors acquire in the course of their work as instructors, advisers, and counselors should be considered confidential. Protection against improper disclosure is a serious professional obligation." In a note, the Joint Statement advises institutions to have policies addressing the protection of student records as addressed in federal law as well as policies and practices to control access to student records in electronic format (American Association of University Professors 2012). Recognizing that respecting library users' privacy is essential to protecting the ability to freely explore information and pursue knowledge (American Library Association 2002), Principle III of the ALA Code of Ethics states: "We protect each library user's right to privacy and confidentiality with respect to information sought or received and resources consulted, borrowed, acquired or transmitted" (American Library Association 2008). The ALA Bill of Rights specifies that this protection applies to all library users, regardless of age: "A person's right to use a library should not be denied or abridged because of origin, age, background, or views" (American Library Association 1996).

Laws are not made in a vacuum. At its best, when it is functioning as intended, the law reflects the values—and thus ethics—of the society it serves. Readers should keep in mind the role of ethics in addressing privacy issues, not only because of a professional duty to abide by one's professional code of ethics, but also because doing so can be a valuable guide in situations where the legal answer may not be clear.

HISTORY OF PRIVACY AS A LEGAL RIGHT

The origin of the concept of a legal right to privacy is widely attributed to the 1890 publication of an article by Samuel Warren and Louis Brandeis (later to become U.S. Supreme Court Justice Brandeis), simply titled "Right to Privacy" (Warren and Brandeis 1890). In this seminal writing, the law partners defined privacy as "the right to be let alone."

The paper was written in response to advances in technology that seemed to "threaten to make good the prediction that 'what is whispered in the closet shall be proclaimed from the house-tops' " (*Id.* [citations omitted]). At the time, "instantaneous cameras"—the first cameras that were capable of taking live-action photographs, as opposed to requiring a subject to sit still for an extended period of time to allow for exposure of the photograph—had become commonplace. As is wont to happen, the media jumped on the new opportunities presented by such technology, one result being the development of an invigorated tabloid press, which regularly published photographs of individuals, without their consent, partaking in private activities; as well as stories about the private lives of individuals (often public figures). At the time, the subjects of such stories had very little, and often no, legal recourse. Warren and Brandeis responded to the accompanying uproar against such offensive invasion of private lives by proposing that individuals have an innate right to control what information, including photographs, about them is made public. The authors reviewed past court cases in which the defendant was accused of breaking a statutory law—such as breaking property laws by stealing documents; or libel, which occurs when publishing false information about an individual; or breach of an implied, unwritten contract—but in which, in all cases, the actual harm done seemed to be beyond the more obvious and tangible acts to which the law was addressed. The greater harms that actually seemed to have occurred, and with which the courts seemed most concerned, appeared to be less about the acts that constituted breaking the law than about hurt feelings, mental distress, and violation of honor. These, the authors concluded, identified rights that, although neither tangible nor clearly protected by law, "are not rights arising from contract or from special trust, but are rights as against the world," a "right of privacy." Such a right, they stated, had impliedly been recognized by the courts for decades, despite such a right not having been clearly and specifically articulated in either statutory or case law (*Id.*).

Warren and Brandeis went on to propose what the structure of such a clearly articulated law should look like. In their proposal, all individuals would have a right to control what information about them is made public, regardless of whether the publicized version of the information is true, and regardless of the motivation of the person making it public. Certain limitations would apply, however. The law would not prevent another from disclosing information about someone if that person had already made the information public in some way, or if the person was a public figure and the information was relevant to the person's public role.

Thus began our move towards creating legal protections for a range of "privacy" rights.

During the twentieth century, the courts developed a body of privacy law that, while solid and expanding, was nonetheless based in a wide variety of statutory laws. In 1960, William Prosser, dean of the University of California at Berkeley College of Law, published his landmark review of over 300 privacy cases decided since the publication of the Warren and Brandeis article (Prosser 1960). As a result of his analysis, Prosser identified four different categories of privacy infringement, later embodied in the Restatement of Torts, the primary treatise on infringement of civil laws:

1. Intrusion—A person's privacy is violated by intrusion when another intentionally invades that person's solitude, seclusion, or private affairs or concerns, whether physically or otherwise, in a manner that would be highly offensive to a reasonable person. In addition to physical invasions, such as forcing oneself into another's home, this would include invasion of another's private affairs, such as peeping into a bedroom window or going through someone's private papers.

2. Appropriation—Appropriation is the use of another's likeness for one's own benefit. "Likeness" refers to a component of one's self that can be used to identify the person, or that brings to mind the person, including names and photographs. In some cases, it may include voice or mannerisms, when specifically associated with that person. Most state laws of appropriation have focused on the "right of publicity," which involves the use of another's likeness for commercial benefit, as in using someone else's image in advertising without their permission.

3. Unreasonable publicity—This term refers to someone who publicizes the private life of another if the matter publicized would be highly offensive to a reasonable person and is not of legitimate concern to the public. For example, publicizing a private citizen's drug addiction might constitute an invasion in this category, but doing the same regarding a candidate for public office may not, because it is in the public's interest to know such information about candidates for public office.

4. False light—Often overlapping with defamation, this category includes acts of publicizing a matter involving someone else when it puts that person in a false

light—that is, creates an inaccurate impression—if doing so would be highly offensive to a reasonable person and the offender acted in reckless disregard as to the falsity and the false light in which the other would be placed. Unlike defamation, an infringement of privacy occurs here regardless of whether the falsehoods caused actual harm to the person (*Id.*).

This categorization of types of privacy has greatly influenced the approach taken in the development of U.S. privacy law, both statutory and case law.

MODERN ARTICULATION OF PRIVACY CONCEPTS

Personally Identifiable Information

The concept of "personally identifiable information" (sometimes referred to as "personally identifying information"), or "PII," forms the basis for much privacy law and regulation regarding the privacy of records, particularly in the online context. The basic concept is that any information or data capable of identifying an individual should be provided certain types of protection. Obvious examples of PII would include name, social security number, and driver's license number. Although the concept seems simple enough, it turns out that determining which data are capable of identifying an individual is not an easy task.

Laws and regulations do not use a uniform definition of PII and, in fact, even take different approaches to how they define PII, each of which has its own problems. Some define PII as "non-public information" but do not explain what that term means. The lack of definition and the shifting boundaries of what constitutes "public" make this definition problematic to rely upon. Others, such as the federal Children's Online Privacy Protection Act, provide a laundry list of specific items that are considered PII, such as name, address, and telephone number. Finally, some legislation defines PII as "information which identifies a person." The last two categories share the same problem, which is explained in the next section, "When 'Anonymous' Doesn't Mean Anonymous."

Today more than ever, we appreciate that information, even raw data, has great financial value. The owners of websites, social media tools, and cell phone applications make millions if not billions of dollars annually on "targeted," or "behavioral," advertising, as they collect bits and pieces of data about us and our online behavior, then use that information to design marketing strategies that will most appeal to each of us, based on our preferences as revealed by our online behavior. These data collectors attempt to assure us that although they collect, share, and use data about us in countless ways, our privacy is protected. They will do their best, they say, to ensure that no one will be able to tie their data about us to our actual identity. Underlying the belief that such protection is possible is the assumption that if we "de-identify," or "anonymize," data, it is impossible to use that data to identify an individual person. A set of data is "anonymized" when it is stripped of any particular data capable of identifying an individual. Indeed, the ability to anonymize underlies the entire concept of PII, which in turn has been the underlying basis of the modern concept of privacy law. The theory goes that if all PII is removed from the data collected about my actions, such as the websites I visit or the terms I enter in a search engine, a data collector can go forward in using the remaining data in whatever way it wishes, including sharing with others, and I will never be identified. But is this true?

When "Anonymous" Doesn't Mean Anonymous

Before we explore studies attempting to answer the question of whether removing PII will truly anonymize data, we should note the obvious: A single data point is worthless, and the more data points, the more valuable a set of data. For example, a useful set of data for a retailer might include the data points of gender, age, income, geographical location, and purchasing habits. It would be useful to this retailer to know that women between the ages of 30 and 40 with an income between $50,000 and $75,000 who live in Austin, Texas, buy an average of three pairs of dress shoes annually. Adding more data points makes this set of data more valuable: Do they buy these shoes online, at a boutique, or at a mall? How much do they spend on the shoes? What time of year do they shop for them? Conversely, a single data point—women—is utterly useless.

Several studies and experiments conducted in the last few years have shown (some unintentionally) the surprising ease with which apparently anonymous data can be "reidentified," that is, combined in a manner that allows identifying individuals to a great degree of certainty. The 2000 study by Latanya Sweeney that is credited with blowing open the door on reidentification showed the results of various combinations of only three of the many elements contained in publicly available census data on every U.S. resident (who completes the decennial census, as required by law). Using data from the 1990 census, this study found that 87 percent of people residing in the United States can be identified using the combination of five-digit ZIP code, birth date, and gender; 53 percent can be identified by the combination of city, birth date, and gender; and 18 percent by the combination of the even larger geographic area of county, birth date, and gender (Sweeney 2000).

Within a few years of publication of this groundbreaking study, the vulnerability of the anonymization of the databases of two major international corporations was proved. In 2006, AOL attempted to contribute to the growing interest in open research by releasing an "anonymized" set of 20 million search queries input by 650,000 users. In the course of anonymizing, however, AOL replaced user-identifying information such as names and IP addresses with unique identifier numbers (Ohm 2010). These numbers were needed, of course, to be able to connect search queries made by the same user for the purpose of researching online behavior. As noted above, a lone data point in the wilderness is of very little, if any, value.

As researchers combed through the data, stories connected to certain numerical identifiers began to develop, one of the most startling being the user who searched for "how to kill your wife" along with phrases such as "pictures of dead people" and "car crash photo." Eventually, one researcher was able to identify an individual by looking at the set of search strings connected by the numerical identifier assigned to her. Those included "homes sold in shadow lake subdivision gwinnett county georgia," "landscapers in Lilburn, Ga," and several searches for people with the last name "Arnold." They identified Thelma Arnold of Lilburn, Georgia, who admitted that she was the author of those searches (*Id.* at 1717).

Later in 2006, Netflix released 100 million records showing how 500,000 users had rated movies over a six-year period. The records included the movie being rated, the rating given, and the date of the rating; although stripped of PII, these records also were assigned identifier numbers unique to the user. Netflix offered a prize of $1 million to the first team that found a way to "significantly improve" the algorithm Netflix uses to recommend movies to users based on their prior ratings of movies they have already seen. Only two weeks later, a team of researchers published results of their ability to reidentify using the Netflix records and a small amount of outside knowledge. In their more thorough research project, they provided several examples. If you know when, within about a two-week range, a friend has rated six movies in the database, you will be able to identify that friend on Netflix 99 percent of the time, thereby allowing you access to every other review posted by that person (Ohm 2010). Given that names are not associated with reviews on the Netflix website, this study uncovers the degree of falseness in our sense of security in our online privacy, even when our names are not directly or publicly linked with our online activities.

The failure of anonymization to protect privacy, combined with the inherent conflict between complete privacy of data and the value or utility of data, has led some privacy experts to conclude that we need to revise our basic approach to privacy protection for data. (See, e.g., Ohm 2010.) The current approach is to define and regulate the use of PII; most current privacy law and regulation is based, to varying degrees, on this concept. However, the failure of anonymization strongly suggests that it is not possible to clearly define PII. A variety of different approaches have been put forth, but their effect remains to be seen. However, this area of study is just one more piece of evidence that determining how to balance individual privacy rights and the rights of information users is a moving target.

Fair Information Practices

We have seen how advances in technology led to the first widely recognized articulation of the need for legal protection of personal privacy. Not surprisingly, another flurry of activity related to privacy protection began in the

1960s and 1970s, as use of computers proliferated. Public concern grew as the federal government, in particular, began to collect increasing amounts of personal information and retain it in computer databases.

The Department of Health, Education, and Welfare established the Advisory Committee on Automated Data Systems in 1972. It responded to the growing concerns by issuing a report titled "Records, Computers and the Rights of Citizens," in which it noted that it was increasingly necessary in the modern world for individuals to provide to large entities, both governmental and nongovernmental, information about themselves over which they lost control once provided. Further, the report noted, the individual was often unable to obtain a copy of the information to ascertain its accuracy or to control its use or further dissemination. In some cases, the individual would not even know such information was being collected and used (U.S. Department of Health, Education, and Welfare 1973). Issuance of the report led Congress to enact the Privacy Act of 1974, which restricts the federal government's ability to collect and use information about individuals (5 U.S.C. §552).

The report recommended the establishment of a Code of Fair Information Practices, incorporating the following principles:

1. There must be no personal data record-keeping systems whose very existence is secret.

2. There must be a way for a person to find out what information about him or her is in a record and how it is used.

3. There must be a way for a person to prevent information about him or her that was obtained for one purpose from being used or made available for other purposes without his or her consent.

4. There must be a way for a person to correct or amend a record of identifiable information about him.

5. Any organization creating, maintaining, using, or disseminating records of identifiable personal data must assure the reliability of the data for its intended use and must take precautions to prevent misuses of the data (U.S. Department of Health, Education, and Welfare 1973).

Privacy law has come increasingly to the forefront not just in the United States, but around the world, often driven by growing commercial activity across international boundaries. During the course of the past 100 years, development of privacy protection frameworks by a handful of international organizations has led to acceptance of a general approach to privacy protection. The Organization for Economic Cooperation and Development's Guidelines Governing the Protection of Privacy and Transborder Data Flows (referred to as the "OECD Guidelines") expands on the principles put forth in the Code of Fair Information Practices and provides a set of standards that have become the core elements of privacy protection as recognized by most countries active in privacy protection. You will see many of these principles reflected in the laws, policies, and guidelines discussed in this book.

1. **Collection Limitation Principle:** There should be limits to the collection of personal data, and any such data should be obtained by lawful and fair means and, where appropriate, with the knowledge or consent of the data subject.

2. **Data Quality Principle:** Personal data should be relevant to the purposes for which they are to be used and, to the extent necessary for those purposes, should be accurate, complete, and kept up to date.

3. **Purpose Specification Principle:** The purposes for which personal data are collected should be specified not later than at the time of data collection; subsequent use should be limited to the fulfillment of those purposes or other purposes that are not incompatible with the original purposes and that are specified on each occasion of change of purpose.

4. **Use Limitation Principle:** Personal data should not be disclosed, made available, or otherwise used for purposes other than those specified in accordance with Principle 3 except: (a) with the consent of the data subject or (b) by the authority of law.

5. **Security Safeguards Principle:** Personal data should be protected by reasonable security safeguards against risks such as loss, unauthorized access, destruction, use, modification, or disclosure of data.

6. **Openness Principle:** There should be a general policy of openness about developments, practices, and policies with respect to personal data. Means should be readily available of establishing the existence and nature of personal data and the main purposes of their use, as well as the identity and usual residence of the data controller.

7. **Individual Participation Principle:** An individual should have the right:
   a. to obtain from a data controller confirmation of whether or not the data controller has data relating to him or her;
   b. to have communicated to him or her: data relating to him or her within a reasonable time; at a charge, if any, that is not excessive; in a reasonable manner; and in a form that is readily intelligible to him or her;
   c. to be given reasons if a request made under subparagraphs (a) and (b) is denied, and to be able to challenge such denial; and
   d. to challenge data relating to him or her and, if the challenge is successful, to have the data erased, rectified, completed, or amended.

8. **Accountability Principle:** A data controller should be accountable for complying with measures that give effect to the principles stated above (OECD 2012).

The OECD Guidelines have become the accepted standard around the world for formulating privacy policies and practices, in both governmental and nongovernmental settings, although specific statements of the principles may differ; and have been incorporated into national law in some jurisdictions, including the European Union.

Choice

A fundamental difference between U.S. privacy law and that of many other countries, including those of the European Union, is the approach to choice. Note that both the Code of Fair Information Practices and the OECD Guidelines give individuals the ability to choose when information about them is collected and/or how it is used and further disseminated. This is called the principle of "choice." In the United States, the typical approach to providing this option is to give the individual the ability to opt out of having his or her PII collected or used in a certain way; in other words, the default is that PII will be collected or used. In contrast, the E.U. Directive requires that the individual opt in before PII is collected or used; the default is that PII is not collected until the individual gives his or her consent.

For example, a Terms of Use statement on a website—to which the vast majority of users agree without reading—may include the following opt-out provision:

> By agreeing to these Terms of Use, you agree that we may share your personal information with our marketing partners. If you do not want us to do this, contact us at optout@company.com.

Another, perhaps more common, example of an opt-out provision occurs on website registration pages, when the page includes a box, already checked, that says, "I want to receive emails about future offerings." The user must uncheck the box to be removed from the mailing list.

The opt-in version of these scenarios would be to provide a blank box to be checked if the user is willing to have his or her information shared or willing to receive emails. The key is whether the individual must take action to be included or take action to be excluded. The opt-out version puts the burden on the individual to protect his or her own privacy.

THE INTERNATIONAL FRONT

Many countries take a more holistic approach to privacy law than does the United States. These countries often provide more stringent protection for PII and personal privacy generallythan does the United States. This difference can create challenging situations in a world defined by global commerce, multinational security issues, and the Internet, where the personal information and documents involved in a single transaction may cross several borders, creating confusion, and often conflict, as to which law(s) apply. Moreover, users—the subjects of that personal information—whose expectations for privacy protection are based on their nation's law and culture often have no idea of what is happening or the implications.

For example, the European Union issued its Data Protection Directive in 1995, imposing much more stringent requirements on those who collect and transfer PII than does U.S. law. The directive continues to evolve as technology evolves. The directive prohibits transfer of PII into or out of the European Union by any party not abiding by the standards of the E.U. Directive. However, recognizing that enforcing this prohibition against U.S. entities would cripple trade between the two, the European Union has established a safe harbor for U.S. entities, which requires following certain procedures and formalities. For more information, see the Department of Commerce website at http://export.gov/safeharbor/eu/eg_main_018475.asp.

BIBLIOGRAPHY

American Association of University Professors, "Joint Statement on Rights and Freedoms of Students," http://www.aaup.org/aaup/pubsres/policydocs/contents/stud-rights.htm (cited November 24, 2012).

American Library Association, "Library Bill of Rights," http://www.ala.org/advocacy/intfreedom/librarybill/ (January 23, 1996).

American Library Association, "Privacy: An Interpretation of the Library Bill of Rights," http://www.ala.org/advocacy/sites/ala.org.advocacy/files/content/intfreedom/librarybill/interpretations/privacyinterpretation.pdf (June 19, 2002).

American Library Association, "Code of Ethics of the American Library Association," http://www.ala.org/advocacy/proethics/codeofethics/codeethics (January 22, 2008).

Gellman, Robert, "Fair Information Practices: A Basic History," http://bobgellman.com/rg-docs/rg-FIPShistory.pdf (November 12, 2012).

National Education Association, "Code of Ethics," http://www.nea.org/home/30442.htm (1975).

OECD, "OECD Guidelines on the Protection of Privacy and Transborder Flows of Personal Data," http://www.oecd.org/internet/interneteconomy/oecdguidelineson theprotectionofprivacyandtransborderflowsofpersonaldata.htm (cited November 17, 2012).

Ohm, Paul, "Broken Promises of Privacy: Responding to the Surprising Failure of Anonymization," 57 *UCLA L. Rev.* 1701 (2010).

Prosser, William L., "Privacy," 48 *Cal. L. Rev.* 383 (1960).

Shelton v. Tucker, 364 U.S. 479, 487 (1960).

Sweeney, Latanya, *Simple Demographics Often Identify People Uniquely* (Pittsburgh: Carnegie Mellon University, 2000).

U.S. Department of Health, Education, and Welfare, "Records, Computers, and the Rights of Citizens," http://epic.org/privacy/hew1973report/default.html (1973).

Warren, Samuel, and Louis D. Brandeis, "Right to Privacy," 4 *Harvard L. Rev.* 193 (1890).

West Virginia State Bd. of Ed. v. Barnette, 319 U.S. 624, 637 (1943).

CHAPTER 2

Statutory Law Most Pertinent to the Educational Context

The United States does not have a single umbrella or overarching privacy statute. Instead, federal law in the United States takes the approach of addressing privacy and related issues in specific contexts. This chapter will provide an overview of those federal statutes most pertinent to educators. In addition, state legislatures may fill in what they perceive as gaps in federal law with their own statutory law. While it is beyond the scope of this book to thoroughly discuss the laws of each of the 50 states, this chapter will discuss the types of relevant laws that typically exist at the state level. This chapter is only an overview of statutory law; you should always consult your institution's legal counsel when making decisions that rely on comprehensive and accurate understanding of the law.

FEDERAL STATUTES

Family Educational Rights and Privacy Act (FERPA): Protecting Student Records

The Family Educational Rights and Privacy Act (FERPA) was passed in 1974 to address growing concerns about the misuse of information contained in student records. Because it applies to any institution receiving funds from the Department of Education, it applies to most private institutions as well as publicly funded institutions. The goals of FERPA are twofold: (1) to ensure that parents of minor students have access to their children's educational records and that students aged 18 and above, and students of higher education regardless of age, have access to their own educational records; and (2) to protect against the sharing of information in those records without obtaining prior consent. Although the major points of FERPA are explained here, some provisions that will not be widely applicable are not discussed here. For the sake of simplification, I will use the term "authorized person" (although the statute does not) to refer to the person or persons to whom FERPA grants the right to access and control student records: In the case of minor students, that is the student's parents or legal guardian; in the case of students aged 18 or older, and postsecondary students of any age, that is the student himself or herself.

FERPA neither requires nor prohibits particular conduct in the sense of assessing penalties or punishment if its provisions are not followed. Rather, enforcement of FERPA is tied to federal funding of educational institutions. Funds from any program administered by the U.S. secretary of education will be denied to any educational institution or agency that does not abide by the regulations put forth by FERPA. Almost all educational institutions, including private ones, receive some kind of federal funding, which would be subject to loss if FERPA is not followed.

FERPA addresses the use of "educational records," which are defined as any document that contains "information directly related to a student" and that is maintained by "an educational agency or institution or a person acting for such agency or institution." The definition expressly does not include records made by an individual and that are not made accessible to anyone other than a substitute (such as a teacher's personal notes that are not shared with anyone else); records made by a law enforcement unit of the school; for former students currently employed by the school, records related specifically to that employment; and for students in an institution of higher education or who are 18 or older, records created or maintained by a physician, psychiatrist, psychologist, or other professional or paraprofessional, when made, maintained, or used in connection with providing treatment to the student and not made available to anyone other than the treating professionals (20 U.S.C. §1232g(a)(4)).

The law provides that authorized persons have the right to inspect and review the student's current and past educational records. (In the case of records that include information about more than one student, information about other students should be redacted.) Furthermore, the law requires each educational institution to implement "appropriate procedures" for granting access to educational records once requested by an authorized person, within a "reasonable" time frame, and no later than 45 days after the request was made. The authorized person must be given an opportunity for a hearing to challenge the content of the records for the purposes of correcting inaccuracies, misleading information, or otherwise inappropriate information; and to have included in the records a written explanation of the same (20 U.S.C. §1232g(a)(1)(A)).

In addition, funds will be withheld from any educational institution that "has a policy or practice" of, without consent of the authorized person, releasing educational records or the personally identifiable information (PII) contained therein (other than directory information, as discussed below) to any individual or entity other than those directly related to the institution or certain entities that collect information regarding studies of education; or in the case of certain emergency situations or court orders (20 U.S.C. §1232g(b)). See Section (b)(1) of FERPA for the detailed list of such entities. When requesting consent to release records beyond these contexts, the request for consent must specify which records will be released and to whom, as well as the reasons for releasing them, and either a copy of the records to be released must be given to the authorized person or arrangements must be made for the authorized person to inspect and review the records. Even then, access can be granted only on the condition that the receiving party not permit any other individual or entity to have access to the records without first obtaining written consent of the authorized person (20 U.S.C. §1232g(b)(2)(A); 34 C.F.R. § 99.10 (2009)). The institution must "effectively" inform the authorized person of these rights (20 U.S.C. §1232g(e)). Note, however, that these requirements under FERPA are trumped by one section of the No Child Left Behind Act of 2002 (see below).

Each educational institution must keep records of all individuals or entities that request, or are given, access to a student's educational records (other than directory information) and indicate any legitimate interest that person or entity has in obtaining the records (20 U.S.C. §1232g(b)(4)(A)).

FERPA also requires that an educational entity that provides directory information to the public must give notice of the categories of information to be included in the directory and provide a reasonable period of time for an authorized person to instruct that some or all of the information not be released (20 U.S.C. §1232g(b)(5)(B)).

FERPA specifies several clarifications and exceptions to its requirements. For students in higher education institutions, the right to view their records does not extend to their parents' financial records. Students can waive their right to access confidential letters of recommendation, but only if, upon request, the student is given a list of the names of everyone making such recommendations and the recommendations are used only for the intended purpose, that is, making decisions about admissions (20 U.S.C. §1232g(a)(1)(C)).

Note that several states have legislation further regulating the collection and use of student data.

The Protection of Pupil Rights Amendment (PPRA): Gathering Student Information in Surveys

The Protection of Pupil Rights Amendment (PPRA), which is applicable to the same institutions as is FERPA, regulates, among other things, the administration of "surveys" to students of all ages. It prohibits, unless prior written consent has been obtained from the parent of a minor or from a student aged 18 or over, requiring students to submit to a survey, analysis, or evaluation that reveals information about any of the following:

- political affiliations or beliefs of the student or the student's parent;
- mental or psychological problems of the student or the student's family;
- sex behavior or attitudes;
- illegal, antisocial, self-incriminating, or demeaning behavior;

- critical appraisals of other individuals with whom respondents have close family relationships;
- legally recognized privileged or analogous relationships, such as those of lawyers, physicians, and ministers;
- religious practices, affiliations, or beliefs of the student or student's parent; or
- income (other than that required by law to determine eligibility for participation in a program or for receiving financial aid under a program) (20 U.S.C. §1232h(b))

In addition, educational institutions must adopt policies regarding protecting the privacy of students who partake in such surveys, including allowing parents to inspect the survey (20 U.S.C. §1232h(c)(1)).

The PPRA also requires notifying parents at least at the beginning of each school year of the specific or approximate dates when any of the following are expected to be scheduled:

- The administration of any survey of the type listed above.
- The collection, disclosure, or use of personal information collected from students for the purpose of marketing or for selling that information.
- The administration of any nonemergency, invasive physical examination or screening that is required as a condition of attendance; administered by the school and scheduled by the school in advance; and not necessary to protect the immediate health and safety of the student, or of other students (20 U.S.C. §1232h(c)(2)).

For more information on FERPA and the PPRA, see the U.S. Department of Education's Family Policy Compliance Office website at http://www2.ed .gov/policy/gen/guid/fpco/index.html.

No Child Left Behind Act (NCLB): Undermining FERPA

Although the No Child Left Behind Act primarily focuses on establishing, meeting, and tracking standards in primary and secondary schools, Section 9528 specifically addresses the disclosure of PII about secondary school students. That provision states that any educational institution receiving federal funding—the same ones subject to FERPA—must, upon request, provide to military recruiters or institutions of higher education, access to students' names, addresses, and telephone numbers. Furthermore, it specifically says that schools must do so despite FERPA requirements. In comparison to FERPA, which essentially follows an "opt-in" procedure whereby the authorized person under FERPA must give consent before such information is disclosed, NCLB includes an "opt-out" provision, whereby either the parent or the student may request that the student's information not be released without specific written consent. The educational institution must inform parents of this option and must comply with any such request (20 U.S.C. §9528).

Children's Online Privacy Protection Act (COPPA): An Attempt to Protect Children Online

COPPA and Educational Institutions

The Children's Online Privacy Protection Act (COPPA) was passed in 2000 to address growing concerns for the need to protect children as they use the Internet. COPPA specifically applies to operators of commercial websites; thus, schools and nonprofit entities are almost always exempt from its coverage. Nonetheless, COPPA does have some value for educators.

COPPA provides certain requirements to be met by operators of commercial websites and online services targeted towards children under the age of 13, or that have actual knowledge that they are collecting personal information from children under the age of 13. COPPA takes the approach of putting fair practices into law, with the addition of the role of parents as the party who must be informed of data collection and use practices.

Among other requirements, COPPA requires website operators to obtain "verifiable" consent of parents before collecting PII from children under the age of 13. Even when COPPA was written and passed, schools were increasingly integrating the Internet into their curricular activities, and, of course, that is more true every school year. Some members of the educational community expressed concern that COPPA's parental consent requirement might inhibit the legitimate, educational use of some Internet resources in the classroom. In response, in its Final Rule on COPPA, the Federal Trade Commission clarified that in such a situation, schools may serve as the parent's agent for purposes of granting consent, if the school first obtains parental authority to do so. This can easily be accomplished by obtaining parental consent at the beginning of each school year for the school to act in this role (Children's Online Privacy Protection Rule, 64 Fed. Reg. 59,887, 59,903 [Nov. 3, 1999] [to be codified at 16 C.F.R. pt. 312]).

Since so many websites used by children are required to abide by COPPA, parents are becoming increasingly familiar with the information and options offered to them by such sites regarding the collection and use of their children's PII. Even though not required to do so by law, it is good policy for educational institutions to enact similar provisions in regard to their own websites and students' use of outside sites. In fact, the Federal Trade Commission (which enforces COPPA and promulgates regulations for applying COPPA) encourages schools to act as if subject to COPPA. (See, e.g., Federal Trade Commission 2008; Federal Trade Commission 2010.)

COPPA's Requirements

COPPA requires operators subject to its rules to do the following:

- Obtain verifiable parental consent prior to collecting PII from children under the age of 13. The FTC has provided various mechanisms that would meet the requirement of consent being "verifiable," such as providing a credit card number (probably the most common means currently used) or receiving from the parent an email with a digital signature or other digital certificate.

- Provide notice to parents about the site's practices regarding collecting data.

- Provide parents the choice of whether their child's data may be disclosed to third parties.

- Provide parents with the ability to access and/or delete their child's PII and to opt out of future uses of the PII or collection of additional PII.

- Maintain the integrity, confidentiality, and security of the PII collected from children.

- Not condition a child's participation in an online activity on the provision of more PII than is reasonably necessary for that participation.

- Post a privacy policy on the site's home page and a link to that policy on every page on which PII is collected. The policy must include: contact information for the site operator; explanation of the type of information collected and how it will be used; whether the PII will be disclosed to third parties and information about such disclosure; statement that no condition may be placed on the disclosure of PII; and an explanation of the parent's final right to remove a child's PII and methods for doing so (15 U.S.C. §6502).

Several states have legislation that also addresses collecting information from minors online.

Electronic Communications Privacy Act (ECPA): A Few Pieces of the Electronic Privacy Protection Puzzle

The Electronic Communications Privacy Act actually consists of three separate acts—the Wiretap Act, the Stored Communications Act, and the Pen Register Act—passed at two different times. Each of these addresses a different type of electronic communication, and each provides a different type of restriction, depending on the type of communication.

The Wiretap Act (WTA) was passed in 1968 as part of the Omnibus Crime Control and Safe Streets Act and is currently incorporated into the ECPA as Title I. The WTA provides the standards the government must follow when tapping a landline phone. Importantly, with some limited exceptions, it requires the government to obtain a warrant before tapping a landline phone. As the wireless industry developed and data transmission became increasingly common, concern grew over the lack of protection for such communications. The Electronic Communications Privacy Act was passed in 1986 to address these concerns (18 U.S.C. §§2510–22). It incorporated the 1968 Wiretap Act into Title I of the ECPA and added the Stored Communications Act (SCA) as Title II and the Pen Register Act as Title III. The ECPA was amended in 1994 and 2001 (the latter as part of the USA PATRIOT Act) but has not been significantly amended since. Needless to say, the ECPA does not address many changes in technology that have occurred in the past decade or more.

Demands for a major revision are growing, but to date, Congress has not been successful in its attempts to pass such legislation.

The ECPA defines three categories of electronic communications, with each receiving a different type of protection. "Wire communications" are those that involve "aural transfers" containing a human voice and that travel through a wire or similar medium. The inclusion of a human voice need only be a minor part of the transmission, and travel via wire need only be part of the transmission's voyage from beginning to end. "Oral communications" are those "uttered by a person" who demonstrates an expectation that the communications will not be subject to interception. "Electronic communications" are defined as all non-wire and non-oral communications (18 U.S.C. §2510).

The Wiretap Act prohibits the intentional interception, use, or disclosure of any wire, oral, or electronic communications in transit; a failed attempt to engage in these activities; and procuring another person to engage in these activities. Note that this prohibition applies only to communications in transit, not stored communications once they have been received. Service providers and others whose course of business involves such activity are excluded. The act also provides procedures for the government to obtain warrants to engage in the otherwise prohibited activity (18 U.S.C. §119).

The Stored Communications Act, as its title suggests, protects communications in storage by prohibiting a provider of an electronic communication service from knowingly divulging to third parties the contents of any communication while in electronic storage. If the government wishes to access the content of such stored communications within the first 180 days of storage, it must first obtain a warrant. However, if the communication has been stored for more than 180 days, the government has the option of meeting a much lower standard by simply stating that facts exist supporting a reasonable belief that the communications are relevant to a criminal investigation; in such case, the government must also provide notice to the subscriber (18 U.S.C.§121).

Note that where an educational institution provides its own communications systems, such as email, it would be considered a service provider for purposes of the WTA and SCA.

The Pen Register Act requires the government to obtain a court order authorizing the use of pen register devices or trap-and-trace devices before implementing them. The standard for obtaining the order is low: The government need only certify that the information likely to be obtained is relevant to an ongoing criminal investigation. Pen register devices are used to capture numbers dialed and related information regarding outgoing phone calls and communications. Trap-and-trace devices capture the numbers and related information from incoming calls and communications (18 U.S.C. §206).

The ECPA is the only federal law addressing the privacy of electronic communications. Not only is the ECPA inconsistent in that it provides different levels of protection for communications in different places of the storage or transmission process, but it is also immediately apparent that the ECPA alone does not address a significant amount of information-generating technology whose use has become commonplace since the ECPA's enactment in 1986. For example, what about the protection of stored personal data other than communications, such as the infinite amount of information shared on social networking platforms, or data we store "in the cloud," by using services such as Google Docs, Dropbox, or Microsoft's SkyDrive? The answer is simply that federal law does not address the vast majority of uses of these technologies.

This creates concerns not only for consumers or information users worried about the security of their personal data and information, but also for businesses who cannot assure their customers that they will be able to protect the customers' privacy, and for all entities who are confused and uncertain about their responsibilities to their communities. A push for revising the ECPA began in earnest in 2010, when privacy advocates and the business community began to work together and with Congress to update the ECPA. Work has been ongoing, and bills have been introduced, but as of the date of this writing, legislative reform is still a good distance off.

As always, keep in mind that some states have statutory law filling in the gaps in federal law. State law may be more restrictive than federal law. However, depending on state law in this context is particularly troublesome since information in electronic format is by definition borderless.

Note that the USA PATRIOT Act, discussed below, overlaps in some areas with the following statutes.

USA PATRIOT Act: Has Big Brother Arrived?

The Uniting and Strengthening America by Providing Appropriate Tools Required to Intercept and Obstruct Terrorism Act of 2001 (USA PATRIOT Act) was passed in response to the September 11, 2001, attacks and greatly expanded already existing national security law. Despite its length and complexities, it was written, passed, and signed into law in only six weeks. As will be discussed throughout this book, all legal rights come with limitations; indeed, one person's rights often equate with the denial of rights to another. The ongoing struggle to balance conflicting rights and needs is at the very basis of U.S. law. Nonetheless, it can hardly be an overstatement to say that, in the context of balancing rights, the USA PATRIOT Act may be the most controversial law passed in modern times. In the case of the USA PATRIOT Act, the balancing act is between national security on one side of the scale and individual rights such as freedom of expression and privacy on the other.

The debate is about how much of each to trade off. If we want greater national security, we must give up some personal freedoms; we agree to be searched before boarding a plane in the hopes that searches will prevent passengers from bringing weapons onto planes. If we want greater civil liberties, we must give up some degree of security; if we are not willing to allow full pat-downs of all plane passengers, we leave open an opportunity for someone to sneak a weapon on board. When the USA PATRIOT Act was reauthorized in 2006, some but not all of the most controversial provisions were modified, although the modifications did not go far enough to please many civil liberty advocates. (See, e.g., Doyle 2002.)

The USA PATRIOT Act was 363 pages long. It both modified existing law and created new law. Several provisions of the USA PATRIOT Act have been strongly criticized for threatening the privacy and/or free speech rights of Americans. This section will discuss in more detail those provisions most applicable to educational institutions and libraries. Others include Section 213, which allows the government, conducting investigations into potential terrorist activities, to conduct searches without providing prior notice and with fewer judicial safeguards than otherwise required under the Fourth Amendment; and Sections 206 and 216, which expand the government's rights to use pen registers, trap-and-trace devices, and wiretaps with less stringent Fourth Amendment guarantees than previous law required, thereby enabling the government to collect more types of information than previously allowed by law, such as Internet usage information.

Underlying the USA PATRIOT Act is an expanded definition of "domestic terrorism" to include activities that

a) involve acts dangerous to human life that are a violation of the criminal laws of the United States or of any state;

b) appear to be intended

  1. to intimidate or coerce a civilian population; or

  2. to influence the policy of a government by intimidation or coercion; or

  3. to affect the conduct of a government by mass destruction, assassination, or kidnapping; and

c) occur primarily within the territorial jurisdiction of the United States (18 U.S.C. §2331).

This is an extraordinarily broad definition that could be used to move various types of civil disobedience commonly occurring in protests from the category of relatively minor criminal activity into the much more serious category of terrorism. (See, e.g., American Civil Liberties Union 2012.)

Of greatest interest to the education community, the act expanded the government's ability to use national security letters (NSLs) and Foreign

Intelligence Surveillance Act (FISA) orders to gather information. Precisely what these tools are and how they can be used, as well as how they differ, has created confusion, even amongst the courts, due to a combination of factors, including the complexity of the act, the historical secrecy shrouding the use of NSLs, abusive use of NSLs, and simply the rhetoric surrounding the entire situation (Nieland 2007, 1207).

National Security Letters

The national security letters process allows the FBI to monitor and collect information without resorting to court approval or oversight. NSLs were originally established in the late 1970s and the 1980s, as amendments to three existing laws regulating the collection and use by the federal government of different types of data, for the purpose of allowing the federal government to more easily obtain data as it deemed necessary for international security purposes. The USA PATRIOT Act greatly expanded the government's ability to use NSLs. As a result of two lawsuits challenging the constitutionality of these provisions, the NSL process drew popular attention for the first time (Nieland 2007, 1202–5). This history has caused some to mistakenly believe that the USA PATRIOT Act established the use of NSLs; in fact, some of the statutory provisions that have been subject to the most vitriolic criticism have been in place for decades. It is true, however, that the use of NSLs skyrocketed after passage of the USA PATRIOT Act, from "hundreds" between 1978 and 2001 to as many as 30,000 or more per year between 2002 and 2005 (*Id.* at 1203).

Prior to the USA PATRIOT Act, the process of using NSLs was limited by what types of information could be requested by them, who could use them, and who could approve them. Before 2001, NSLs could be used to obtain only certain types of information, and then only if the information related to a foreign power: financial records of financial institutions; limited consumer information from consumer reporting agencies; subscriber, billing, and transactions records from wire or electronic service providers; and any of these records from any of these types of institutions if for the purpose of conducting background checks of government employees or investigating them when suspected of spying for foreign powers. NSLs could be used only by the FBI and were issued and approved only by the FBI; no court oversight was involved (18 U.S.C. 2709 (2000); 12 U.S.C. 3414(a)(5) (2000); 15 U.S.C. 1681u–1681v (1998); 50 U.S.C. 436(a) (2000)).

Prior to passage of the act, the FBI had to state "specific and articulable facts giving reason to believe" that the person or entity whose records were sought was a foreign power or agent thereof. After the act, NSLs may be used to obtain information that is merely "relevant to an authorized investigation to protect against international terrorism or clandestine intelligence activities," so long as the investigation is either not of a person of the United States or, if so, is not based on activities protected by the First Amendment. This means that NSLs may be used to obtain information about and from individuals who themselves are not the subject of investigations.

The act also opened up the categories of who may obtain and approve an NSL. NSLs may now be obtained not only by the FBI but, in the case of obtaining consumer credit reports, by any agency authorized to conduct investigations of international terrorism. In addition, whereas approval previously could be granted only by senior FBI officials, special agents in charge of any of the FBI's 56 field offices may now authorize NSLs.

Note that as the final edits of the manuscript were being made, a federal district court in northern California held the statutory provisions governing NSLs, including their gag orders, to be unconstitutional.

Foreign Intelligence Surveillance Act Court Warrants

FISA Court warrants, also referred to as "FISA orders," are often confused with NSLs, and with good reason: their authority overlaps, and much of the procedure associated with both is the same. However, they differ in significant ways. Whereas NSLs may be used to obtain only certain types of records, "any tangible thing" may be obtained by a FISA order, although the government must meet more strenuous requirements to obtain a FISA warrant.

The FISA was originally passed in 1978 and has been amended several times since. It established Foreign Intelligence Surveillance Courts, a court system through which the government can secretly obtain warrants to conduct electronic surveillance for purposes of collecting foreign intelligence. The requirements to obtain a FISA order are lower than what would be required by the Fourth Amendment to obtain a search warrant in criminal investigations. As is true with NSLs, the USA PATRIOT Act greatly expanded the government's ability to use FISA orders, as well the type of information that may be collected by them.

Prior to the act, to obtain a FISA warrant, the government was required to state in the application for an order that "specific and articulable facts" existed that provided a reason to believe that the individual to whom the records pertained was an agent of a foreign power (18 U.S.C. §1862, 2000). A FISA order allowed the government to seize only records of common carriers, public accommodation facilities, physical storage facilities, and car rental facilities (50 U.S.C. §1862, 2000). After the USA PATRIOT Act, FISA allowed the seizure of not just records, but "any tangible thing," and not just from agents of foreign powers, but from "any business or entity," so long as they were being seized for a FISA-authorized investigation "to obtain foreign intelligence information not concerning a United States person" or for the purpose of "protect[ing] against international terrorism or clandestine intelligence activities" (50 U.S.C. §1861).

Amendments Allow Recipients to Object

In the reauthorization of the USA PATRIOT Act, Congress made several amendments in an attempt to address the concerns of privacy and other civil rights advocates. As a result of the amendments, the recipient of an NSL or FISA order now has the right to petition a district court to have the order either set aside or modified, if the order or portions thereof are "unreasonable, oppressive, or otherwise unlawful" (50 U.S.C. §1861, 18 U.S.C. §3511).

Both NSLs and FISA orders automatically have nondisclosure orders attached, which prohibit the recipient from disclosing the fact that he or she has received the NSL. This "gag" order provision also was revised in the reauthorization to allow that, one year after receiving the NSL or FISA order, the recipient may appeal to the court to remove the gag order; however, if the government certifies that there is reason to believe disclosure of the NSL or FISA order "may endanger the national security of the United States or interfere with diplomatic relations," the gag order is renewed, and the recipient must wait one more year before appealing it. The reauthorization also clarified that the gag order allows the recipient to discuss the matter with an attorney; under the original USA PATRIOT Act, even the right to consult an attorney had been unclear. A recipient of an NSL or FISA order who fails to comply may be held in contempt of court, which can bring both financial penalties and imprisonment of up to five years (50 U.S.C. §1861, 18 U.S.C. §3511).

In a nutshell, the USA PATRIOT Act expanded law about which civil rights advocates already had concerns into law allowing the government to collect any tangible item from any person, so long as the government states that its investigation has something to do with national security; and to keep the person from disclosing such actions; and to do so without the constitutional protections afforded to criminal suspects. Among the most vocal of critics was the American Library Association, which argued that the government's ability to secretly seize the records of library users without having to show probable cause, or even to state that the person is a criminal suspect, invades the privacy and First Amendment rights of information users by creating a chilling effect on their information-seeking and use activities. (As discussed below, the right to receive information has been specifically recognized by the Supreme Court as a First Amendment right, implicating both privacy and free speech rights.)

STATE STATUTES

It is well beyond the scope of this book to attempt to address the laws of each of the 50 states. This section will discuss generally the types of relevant law typical amongst the majority of states. Many states may have laws on the books relevant to the topics discussed in this book, beyond those described in this chapter.

As previously noted, where federal and state law conflict, federal law trumps, or "preempts," state law. However, states may create statutory law on the same topics as existing federal law, so long as the state laws do not contradict federal law. Conflict exists when it is impossible to comply with both laws; or when the state law constitutes an obstacle to "the accomplishment and execution of the full purposes and objectives of" the federal law (*Crosby v. National Foreign Trade Council*, 530 U.S. 363, 372–73 (2000)). If federal law grants a right, state law may not restrict the extent of that right. Likewise, if federal law restricts a certain act, state law may not allow that same act.

At the time of this writing, many privacy-related topics are being debated by both state legislatures and Congress. It is entirely possible that, by the time you read this book, some additional statutes will have been passed and current statutes amended, particularly regarding the host of situations involving privacy concerns in the online context. For these reasons, you should consult your institution's legal counsel to confirm your understanding of the law as it applies to any particular situation.

Cyberbullying, Cyberstalking, and Cyberharassment

The terms "cyberbullying," "cyberstalking," and "cyberharassment" have no widely applicable legal definitions, and they are often used interchangeably. Typically, however, "cyberbullying" is used in the context of behavior involving minors. "Stalking" and "harassment" are defined in the statutory laws of each state, with stalking usually being a felony offense generally requiring the existence of reasonable fear in response to a threat, whereas harassment is often a misdemeanor offense of intentionally bothering or causing trouble for someone. In the educational context, these behaviors may involve interactions between students or between a student and a faculty or staff member.

All 50 states have laws addressing stalking and harassment. Some incorporate language specifically addressing engaging in these behaviors in an online or digital arena. As of November 2012, 49 of the 50 states have statutes addressing bullying. Although only 16 use the term "cyberbullying," 47 include provisions addressing electronic harassment, which may equate with bullying. Note that all 49 states require primary and secondary schools to have a policy on bullying, and all but 6 allow for sanctions against the school. The particulars of the laws vary greatly. Some are rather open-ended, simply requiring school boards to adopt policies prohibiting bullying. Some attempt to regulate student behavior outside of the school context, particularly regarding online bullying (Hinduja and Patchin 2012). Thus, educational institutions should be not only knowledgeable of the applicable state law, but also mindful of the intersection with the privacy rights of students, faculty, and staff.

Library Records

The Supreme Court has held in several cases that the First Amendment protects "the right to receive information and ideas" (*Board of Educ., Island Trees*

Union Free Sch. Dist. v. Pico, 457 U.S. 853 (1982)). Further, it has recognized the chilling effect on that right that may occur absent privacy protections: "In a democratic society privacy of communication is essential if citizens are to think and act creatively and constructively. Fear or suspicion that one's speech is being monitored by a stranger, even without the reality of such activity, can have a seriously inhibiting effect upon the willingness to voice critical and constructive ideas" (*Bartnicki v. Vopper*, 532 U.S. 514 (2001)). This is why the American Library Association places such a strong emphasis on protecting the privacy of library users' behavior in seeking and using information.

As a result, 48 of the 50 states have statutes providing some level of protection to library records. Often, this is in the form of an exemption to the state's Open Records Act or Freedom of Information Act. Under those statutes, the public has a right to inspect state records. However, these statutes always exempt certain categories of records, which may include library records. Other states have statutes specific to library records.

The general goal of these statutes is to prevent the disclosure of library use records of all sorts, including circulation records, Internet usage, and reference or consultation activities. Regardless of the nature of the statutory protection, the specifics will differ, including what types of information in a user's record may not be revealed and whether a library is required to provide the records of minors to their parents upon request. Thus, it is vital that all library staff and the relevant institutional administrators understand their own state law on this issue. For a collection of pertinent state laws, see the American Library Association's Office for Intellectual Freedom's website at www.ala.org/offices/oif/ifgroups/stateifcchairs/stateifcinaction/stateprivacy.

The Privacy Torts

A tort is a "private or civil wrong or injury . . . for which the court will provide a remedy in the form of an action for damages" (Black's 1991, 1036). Recall from the discussion in Chapter 1 that the law of privacy has developed into four distinct categories of privacy invasion. Each of these is a privacy tort: invasion by intrusion; appropriation of another's likeness; publicizing the private affairs of another; and publicly portraying another in a false light. These torts are all matters of state law. Most states provide statutory law addressing one or more of these torts. The laws will define precisely what constitutes the tort in that state as well as the remedies, or damages, available to the plaintiff. In most cases, monetary damages are available. Depending on the law, the plaintiff may have to prove that he or she was financially injured by the violation of his or her privacy, which may be in the form of actual loss of money or in the form of emotional distress. Some include the option for punitive damages.

The Right of Publicity

Most states recognize some variation of the right of publicity, also referred to as appropriation of likeness; in some states, the laws are structured as a subset of right of privacy torts. These laws usually protect against the unauthorized commercial use of any individual's "likeness," which includes name, photographs, or any trait that is distinctly associated with that person. Although most educational institutions might assume, without giving much consideration, that all their activities are noncommercial, this is not necessarily true for purposes of these laws. For example, using the image of a celebrity to promote a school fund-raising event could be considered an infringement of that person's right of publicity. Note, however, that where state law allows, the right belongs to everyone, not only famous or well-known individuals.

Mandatory Reporting of Child Abuse

Forty-eight states mandate reporting by designated professionals, often including teachers and other education professionals, of suspected child abuse or neglect. Requirements vary from state to state regarding, among other things, the level of suspicion or knowledge that activates the statutory requirement to report suspected abuse, the confidentiality of the reporter, and the immunity of the reporter to civil and/or criminal liability (Child Welfare Information Gateway 2010). While the dire importance of preventing child abuse and helping its victims should never be minimized, educational employees should be knowledgeable about their own state's laws and mindful of the privacy rights and concerns of all parties involved.

Privacy in Employment Law

Most states have passed statutes addressing privacy in the workplace. The extensiveness of these laws varies, as does the general approach as to whether the employee or the employer is more greatly favored. These laws may cover issues such as monitoring employee workspace visually or aurally; recording employees in the workplace; and accessing employee email. Most recently, several states have moved to pass legislation prohibiting employers from requiring that prospective employees provide login information for their social networking accounts. See Chapter 7 for more discussion on employee privacy rights.

CASE LAW AND OTHER AREAS

All state statutory law includes laws addressing privacy in various contexts; some common areas include identity theft, security of children online, and the publicizing of crime victims' identities. Even situations addressed by federal laws discussed in this book may also be addressed by state law. Furthermore, federal laws—including constitutional law—may be interpreted differently in the same context by different courts. Therefore, before relying on any statement of law found in this book, be sure you know what the law of your state is, and consult your institution's legal counsel as appropriate.

BIBLIOGRAPHY

American Civil Liberties Union, "National Security Letters," http://www.aclu.org/national-security-technology-and-liberty/national-security-letters (January 10, 2011).

American Civil Liberties Union, "How the USA PATRIOT Act Redefines 'Domestic Terrorism,'" http://www.aclu.org/national-security/how-usa-patriot-act-redefines-domestic-terrorism (cited November 10, 2012).

Bartnicki v. Vopper, 532 U.S. 514 (2001).

Black's Law Dictionary, 6th ed. (St. Paul, MN: West Group, 1991).

Board of Educ., Island Trees Union Free Sch. Dist. v. Pico, 457 U.S. 853 (1982).

Children's Online Privacy Protection Rule, 64 Fed. Reg. 59,887, 59,903 (Nov. 3, 1999) (to be codified at 16 C.F.R. pt. 312).

Child Welfare Information Gateway, "Mandatory Reporters of Child Abuse and Neglect: Summary of State Laws," http://www.childwelfare.gov/systemwide/laws_policies/statutes/manda.cfm (April 2010).

Crosby v. National Foreign Trade Council, 530 U.S. 363 (2000).

Doyle, Charles, *The USA PATRIOT Act: A Sketch* (Washington, D.C.: CRS Report for Congress, 2002).

Federal Trade Commission, "Frequently Asked Questions about the Children's Online Privacy Protection Rule," http://www.ftc.gov/privacy/coppafaqs.shtm (October 7, 2008).

Federal Trade Commission, "How to Protect Kids' Privacy Online: A Guide for Teachers," http://www.ftc.gov/bcp/edu/pubs/consumer/tech/tec10.shtm (December 2010).

Hinduja, Sameer, and Justin W. Patchin, "State Cyberbullying Laws," http://www.cyberbullying.us/Bullying_and_Cyberbullying_Laws.pdf (November 2012).

Liu, Edward C., "Amendments to the Foreign Intelligence Surveillance Act (FISA) Extended Until June 1, 2015," http://www.fas.org/sgp/crs/intel/R40138.pdf (June 16, 2011).

National Conference of State Legislatures, "State Cyberstalking and Cyberharassment Laws," http://www.ncsl.org/issues-research/telecom/cyberstalking-and-cyberharassment-laws.aspx (November 16, 2012).

Nieland, Andrew. "National Security Letters and the Amended Patriot Action," 92 *Cornell L. Rev.* 1201 (2007).

United States Department of Justice, Office of Justice Programs, "Federal Statutes Relevant in the Information Sharing Environment," http://www.it.ojp.gov/default.aspx?area=privacy&page=1285 (November 17, 2012).

CHAPTER 3

Constitutional Law

The U.S. Constitution does not provide a right of privacy per se. However, various privacy rights have been found in the Constitution, primarily in the First and Fourth Amendments, which state as follows:

> **Amendment I:** Congress shall make no law respecting an establishment of religion, or prohibiting the free exercise thereof; or abridging the freedom of speech, or of the press; or the right of the people peaceably to assemble, and to petition the Government for a redress of grievances.
>
> **Amendment IV:** The right of the people to be secure in their persons, houses, papers, and effects, against unreasonable searches and seizures, shall not be violated, and no Warrants shall issue, but upon probable cause, supported by Oath or affirmation, and particularly describing the place to be searched, and the persons or things to be seized.

The Constitution and its amendments grant powers to, and limit the powers of, government. Originally, the Constitution applied only to the federal government. However, after decades of debate, the Supreme Court now considers that most provisions of the Bill of Rights extend also to state governments and their agents. Public school districts, boards, and officials are considered to be government agencies for purposes of applying constitutional law (*New Jersey v. T.L.O.*, 469 U.S. 325, 336 (1985)).

Because the Constitution itself provides both the source of government authority and limitations on that authority, the interpretation and application of constitutional law is, in its simplest form, about finding and maintaining that balance. The government clearly has both the authority and duty to protect its citizenry. Adjudication of the Fourth Amendment is about finding the balance between granting the government the authority to conduct investigations of criminal activity and other misconduct, for the purpose of protecting the people, and restraining the government from overextending its actions, also for the purpose of protecting the people. Application of the First Amendment is about finding the balance between restricting the government's ability to prevent the people from, among other rights, speaking freely and openly, for the purpose of protecting and growing a healthy society, and applying some limits when necessary for the purpose of protecting society from a variety of threats. In this context, the Supreme Court famously said, "The most stringent protection of free speech would not protect a man in falsely shouting fire in a theatre and causing a panic" (*Schenck v. United States*, 249 U.S. 47, 52 (1919)).

Because many of our constitutional rights are so fundamentally a part of our lives and our self-identity as a society, we often fall into the trap of assuming that they apply to all parts of our life. For that reason, it is important to keep in mind that constitutional limitations apply only to governmental entities, not private parties. Therefore, while other laws may prohibit someone not an agent of the government from "unreasonable search and seizure," the Fourth Amendment does not. Likewise, while government entities are prohibited by the First Amendment from restricting the right of individuals to freely express themselves, private entities are not. Most state tort law regarding invasion of privacy is based on the concepts fleshed out in Fourth Amendment case law, so the following should be valuable to those working in private educational institutions as well as public.

Also note that although most case law addressing these issues in the educational context involves primary and secondary educational institutions, the standards and holdings are usually applicable in the higher education context as well. This is because the broader basis for analysis in these areas is the determination of what is reasonable in the specific context in which the case arises. Thus, the standards used to judge the constitutionality of the defendant's actions will be the same, but the analysis will differ depending on the particular facts of the situation, including the level of the institution and the age of any students involved.

FOURTH AMENDMENT: REASONABLE SEARCH AND SEIZURE

The Fourth Amendment recognizes that situations do occur in which the government needs to conduct searches or seizures of private property and private areas, and it provides protection to the individual whose privacy is thus invaded. The Fourth Amendment protects the privacy of our homes, our bodies, and our possessions from being unreasonably searched or taken by the government. It also requires that any warrants issued by the government authorizing a search or a seizure of property must describe in detail what is to be searched or confiscated; and that to obtain a warrant, the government must first show that it has probable cause to conduct the search or seizure.

When a plaintiff complains that his or her Fourth Amendment rights have been infringed, the court goes through a multistep process in determining if the Fourth Amendment applies to the situation, and if so, whether the plaintiff's rights have indeed been infringed. The key to application of the Fourth Amendment is "reasonableness."

First, the court will consider whether the government's actions actually constitute a search or seizure under the Fourth Amendment. To fit into the Fourth

Amendment, the person subject to the search or seizure must have a "reasonable" expectation of privacy, based on his or her own behavior as well as society's expectations under the circumstances in which the search or seizure occurred (*Katz v. United States*, 389 U.S. 347 (1967)). Observing something in plain view does not constitute a search under the Fourth Amendment, because no reasonable expectation of privacy exists in such situations. Examples of a search as defined by the Fourth Amendment include looking inside an individual's purse or pockets, opening closed communications, entering closed space such as an office or home, and searching a person's body (including clothing). A seizure occurs when a government official takes physical control of an item or a person. The "seizure" of a person under the Fourth Amendment occurs when "a reasonable person would have believed that he was not free to leave" (*Michigan v. Chesternut*, 486 U.S. 567, 573 (1988)).

Assuming that a search or seizure for Fourth Amendment purposes has occurred, the court will then consider whether the government was reasonable in conducting it. Reasonableness is determined by the totality of the circumstances, and different standards are applied in making the analysis, depending on the context.

The standard the government must meet to conduct a search or seizure in a criminal context is generally the highest. This is because the potential repercussions in this context are so serious, so we want to be sure that the individual is sufficiently protected. Usually, a warrant is required. To obtain a warrant, the government must show to a court that probable cause for the search or seizure exists. The Supreme Court has defined probable cause as existing "where known facts and circumstances, of a reasonably trustworthy nature, are sufficient to justify a man of reasonable caution or prudence in the belief that a crime has been or is being committed" (*Draper v. United States*, 358 U.S. 307 (1959)). The threshold for probable cause is higher than simple suspicion. For example, the following have been held not to rise to the level of probable cause: nervousness, fidgeting, or ambiguous gestures on the part of the suspect; possession of a certain kind of envelope, film canister, or other package commonly used to conceal narcotics; and display of certain bumper stickers (Rapp 2012, §9.08).

Even if probable cause does not exist, a search may be held to be constitutional if "special needs, beyond the normal need for law enforcement, make the warrant and probable-cause requirement impracticable" (*New Jersey v. T. L. O.*, 469 U.S. 325, 351 (1985)). The special-needs doctrine applies only when the search is not conducted for law enforcement purposes. Even in such special needs circumstances, however, whether a search is valid is judged on how reasonable it is, based on an assessment of all the circumstances. The court must balance the needs of the government with the degree to which the individual's privacy has been invaded. The more serious the suspected infraction by the individual, the more invasive the government's actions may be. Thus, whereas a strip search of a student accused of carrying cheat notes for an exam clearly would be considered unreasonable, a strip search of a student suspected of carrying a gun is more likely to be considered reasonable. In the educational context, the Supreme Court has articulated the reasonableness standard for a search as requiring that the search have been justified at its inception and reasonable in scope considering the circumstances (*Id.*). Although the high court has not defined a standard for seizures in the educational context, many lower courts apply the same standard. This is discussed in greater detail below.

Some factors to consider in determining reasonableness in the educational context include the nature of the alleged infraction; the prevalence of the problem at the school; and the student's age, mental capacity, gender, and disciplinary record. This is not an exhaustive list but reflects some of the factors most noted by the courts (Rapp 2012, §9.08).

A search is also considered to be reasonable if consent is given, although the consent must be freely given. If a student consents to a search, regardless of the nature of the search (the student's person or his or her possessions, or even a strip search), the search will be deemed reasonable. Note that consent can only be granted when the student reasonably believes he or she has the option to refuse to give consent; a substantial body of case law has developed in considering what constitutes voluntary consent. Whether the consent given is truly voluntary should be based on an analysis of the circumstances, including the student's age, mental capacity, and education; whether the student understands his or her rights; whether the student has been subject to any coercion or duress; and the length and nature of detention when the student is questioned (Rapp 2012,§8.01). Thus, the analysis will be very different for a 10-year-old fourth grader than for a 20-year-old college student. As one court has summarized: "Consent must be proved by clear and positive testimony and must be unequivocal, specific, and intelligently given, uncontaminated by any duress and coercion. Consent must not be coerced, by explicit or implicit means, by implied threat, or covert force. When conducting this analysis, account must also be taken for the potentially vulnerable subjective state of the searched person" (*Fewless v. Board of Educ.*, 208 F. Supp. 2d 806, 813 (W.D. Mich. 2002)).

Courts have held that consent to a search was not voluntary when a high school student was questioned by both the principal and a police officer and was twice threatened with arrest and calling in his uncle who was a police officer (*M.J. v. State of Florida*, 399 So. 2d 996 (1981)); and when a disabled high school student said he had "nothing to hide" and was then told that he could be searched by either school officials or four police officers standing outside (*Fewless*, 208 F. Supp. 2d 806).

Keep in mind that the scope of any search must be both "reasonably related to the objectives of the search" and "not excessively intrusive in light of the age and sex of the student and the nature of the infraction" (*New Jersey v. T.L.O.*, 469 U.S. 325 (1985)).

FIRST AMENDMENT: INTERTWINED WITH RIGHT OF PRIVACY

The First Amendment to the Constitution grants several types of protection from government intrusion: the right to practice the religion of one's choice; the right to speak freely and openly; the right of the press to publish without government censorship; the right to publicly gather in groups, so long as peace is maintained; and the right to complain without retribution to the government when one has been wronged (U.S. Const. amend. I). The concept of free speech is so deeply engrained in our society that we sometimes make the leap to believing that we pretty much have the right to say anything, anytime, anywhere. This is not the case. First Amendment law has developed to provide greater protection to certain types of speech than others, reflecting the values of our society. For example, political speech is among the types of speech most highly protected, and whereas purely commercial speech—speech that is "related solely to the economic interests of the speaker and its audience"— once received no First Amendment protection, it is now allowed a limited degree of protection (*Rubin v. Coors Brewing Co.*, 514 U.S. 476, 545–46 (1995)). The First Amendment governs only restrictions by the government on our ability to express ourselves freely, not restrictions on private parties. Thus, for example, private schools are able to regulate speech and expression in manners and degrees that public schools cannot. And, as we shall see, different levels of protection are provided in different contexts; speech that cannot be restricted in a true public forum may be regulated in an educational setting.

Although a right of privacy is not expressly granted in the Constitution, the concept is deeply ingrained in and intertwined with several amendments, including the first. First Amendment law is a broad and complex area of law, and it has a multitude of applications in the educational context. It is discussed here because, and only to the extent that, it intersects with the right of privacy.

The Supreme Court has made clear in several cases that students have a constitutional right to freedom of expression in the educational setting: "[Students] cannot be punished merely for expressing their personal views on the school premises—whether 'in the cafeteria, or on the playing field, or on the campus during the authorized hours,'—unless school authorities have reason to believe that such expression will 'substantially interfere with the work of the school or impinge upon the rights of other students' " (*Hazelwood Sch. Dist. v. Kuhlmeier*, 484 U.S. 260, 267 (1988), quoting *Tinker v. Des Moines Indep. Cmty. Sch. Dist.*, 393 U.S. 503 at 509, 512–13 (1969)).

Because freedom of speech is considered to be a fundamental right, limiting or prohibiting that right can only be justified if doing so serves an important and valuable government purpose. The basis of First Amendment law is finding the balance between the individual's right to free speech and the need for government to, on occasion, restrict free speech to meet its own obligations and responsibilities to the citizenry. In the analysis, the weight given to each side of the scale varies according to the other: Where the type of speech is most highly protected, the standard that the government must meet in showing the importance of its restriction on the speech is also extremely high.

Given our country's history, it should be of no surprise that government attempts to regulate speech based on its content are regarded by the courts with great trepidation. Where government prohibitions on speech are "content-based"—meaning that they restrict a particular message—the court will apply a higher level of scrutiny, meaning that the government interest being furthered by the restriction must be very important. Within the category of content-based restrictions, prohibition of speech expressing a particular viewpoint is especially disfavored by the courts. In contrast, if the prohibited expression is "content-neutral," it is more likely to be upheld. (See, e.g., Farber 2003, 22–38.) For example, an institution's policy forbidding students to wear T-shirts with any type of political expression would be content-based, but viewpoint-neutral. A policy forbidding students to wear T-shirts expressing opposition to a particular political issue would be viewpoint-based. In contrast, a policy prohibiting T-shirts with any writing on them at all would be content-neutral.

The four U.S. Supreme Court cases addressing First Amendment rights in the public education context provide a good demonstration of how a court approaches this analysis.

Tinker v. Des Moines Independent Community School District, 393 U.S. 503 (1969): The Supreme Court Affirms Student Right of Free Speech

Tinker was the first Supreme Court case to affirm student rights of free speech. In it, the Court confirmed that students have a First Amendment right to free speech and held that any speech restrictions by a school must be based on evidence of actual harm or an established likelihood of harm resulting from the speech, such as disruption in the classroom, not just the unproven potential of harm; and that, absent rare circumstances requiring an exception, the restrictions must be viewpoint-neutral (*Tinker v. Des Moines Indep. Cmty. Sch. Dist.*, 393 U.S. 503 (1969)).

The plaintiffs in this case were two high school students and the junior high school sister of one. They were part of a group of adults and children, including their own parents, who decided to demonstrate their opposition to the Vietnam War by wearing black armbands throughout the holiday season. When the principals of their schools learned of the plan, they adopted a policy that any student wearing an armband would be told to remove it, and, if he or she refused, would be suspended until he or she returned to school without the armband. The students then attended class wearing the armbands and were suspended. They filed suit, alleging violation of their First Amendment rights (*Id.*).

At trial, the school district argued that its policy was necessary to prevent disruption in the classroom and learning environment. The Supreme Court began by noting that neither students nor teachers "shed their constitutional rights to freedom of speech or expression at the school house gate" (*Id.* at 506). On the other hand, the Court said, the law also clearly provides "comprehensive authority" to school officials "consistent with fundamental constitutional safeguards, to prescribe and control conduct in the schools" (*Id.* at 507). Noting that the plaintiffs' actions had been merely silent, passive expressions of their opinion and had not caused any disruption or disorder in the schools, the Court eloquently explained that mere fear or expectation of a disturbance is not sufficient to overcome fundamental First Amendment rights:

Any departure from absolute regimentation may cause trouble. Any variation from the majority's opinion may inspire fear. Any word spoken, in class, in the lunchroom, or on the campus, that deviates from the views of another person may start an argument or cause a disturbance. But our Constitution says we must take this risk; and our history says that it is this sort of hazardous freedom—this kind of openness—that is the basis of our national strength and of the independence and vigor of Americans who grow up and live in this relatively permissive, often disputatious, society (*Id.* at 508–9 [citations omitted]).

The Court also pointed out that the school district did not prohibit wearing all symbols of political or controversial significance, which indicates that its actual purpose was to suppress the particular message those students conveyed, or perhaps to avoid controversy; but not, as had been argued, to control discipline in the school setting (*Id.* at 510–11).

Holding that the students' First Amendment rights had been infringed, the Court said:

[Students] are possessed of fundamental rights which the State must respect, just as they themselves must respect their obligations to the State. In our system, students may not be regarded as closed-circuit recipients of only that which the State chooses to communicate. They may not be confined to the expression of those sentiments that are officially approved. In the absence of a specific showing of constitutionally valid reasons to regulate their speech, students are entitled to freedom of expression of their views. [S]chool officials cannot suppress "expressions of feelings with which they do not wish to contend" (*Id.* at 512 [citations omitted]).

Bethel School District No. 403 v. Fraser, 478 U.S. 675 (1986): The Constitutional Rights of Students Are Not Automatically Equivalent to Those of Adults

The *Bethel* Court held that the constitutional rights of students are not automatically equivalent to those of adults in nonschool settings and held constitutional a student's suspension, based on its findings that his speech was viewpoint-neutral, harmful to young people, and occurred in an official school setting (*Bethel Sch. Dist. No. 403 v. Fraser*, 478 U.S. 675 (1986)).

The plaintiff, a top student but also a class clown, was punished for including in his speech at an official school assembly "highly offensive lewd and indecent speech" (*Id.* at 685). Fraser gave the following speech nominating a friend for school government office:

> I know a man who is firm—he's firm in his pants, he's firm in his shirt, his character is firm—but most ... of all, his belief in you, the students of Bethel, is firm. Jeff Kuhlman is a man who takes his point and pounds it in. If necessary, he'll take an issue and nail it to the wall. He doesn't attack things in spurts—he drives hard, pushing and pushing until finally—he succeeds. Jeff is a man who will go to the very end—even the climax, for each and every one of you. So vote for Jeff for A.S.B. vice-president—he'll never come between you and the best our high school can be (*Id.* at 687 [Brennan, J., concurring]).

The school responded by suspending Fraser and banning him from giving a graduation speech. When Fraser sued, the Supreme Court ruled that the school had not violated his First Amendment rights and emphasized the differences between this case and *Tinker*. The objectives of a public school system rightly include teaching not only subject matter found in books and the curriculum, the Court said, but also "fundamental values necessary to the maintenance of a democratic political system," which include consideration of the sensibilities of others. "The undoubted freedom to advocate unpopular and controversial views in schools and classrooms must be balanced against the society's countervailing interest in teaching students the boundaries of socially appropriate behavior. Even the most heated political discourse in a democratic society requires consideration for the personal sensibilities of the other participants and audiences" (*Id.* at 681). The Court pointed out that Fraser's speech actually had offended many of the students and teachers. Unlike *Tinker*, the speech at issue here did not express any political viewpoint, and did indeed undermine the school's basic educational mission. Thus, the school district's actions were entirely proper (*Id.* at 685).

Hazelwood School District v. Kuhlmeier, 484 U.S. 260 (1988): Schools May Censor Content of School-Sponsored Activities

Kuhlmeier was the first Supreme Court case to analyze the First Amendment in the context of a high school newspaper. Again distinguishing *Tinker*, the Court concluded that a school does not infringe on student First Amendment rights by censoring the content of school-sponsored activities: "[T]he standard articulated in *Tinker* for determining when a school may punish student expression need not also be the standard for determining when a school may refuse to lend its name and resources to the dissemination of student expression. Instead, we hold that educators do not offend the First Amendment by exercising editorial control over the style and content of student speech in school-sponsored expressive activities so long as their actions are reasonably related to legitimate pedagogical concerns" (*Hazelwood Sch. Dist. v. Kuhlmeier*, 484 U.S. 260, 272–73 (1988)).

The high school newspaper was written and produced by the Journalism II class. The standard procedure was for the journalism teacher to take the final proof of the paper to the principal for his approval before publishing. Just before the end of the school year, however, the journalism teacher resigned, and another teacher stepped in to finish the term, causing some delays. When the principal reviewed the last issue, he objected to two stories. The first was about pregnant students and interviewed several; although they were not identified by name, the principal was concerned that enough information was disclosed to allow discovery of their identities. The second article was about divorce. One student interviewed, who was identified by name, complained about her father's behavior. The principal believed that the parents should have been given the opportunity to read the story and, if they so desired, to have their own responses included in the story. Because of the delays, the principal believed that there was not time to edit the stories and still get the paper out before the end of the year. Given the options of either not printing the issue or printing it absent those two stories, the principal chose to omit the stories. Three student members of the paper sued, alleging infringement of their First Amendment rights (*Id.* at 262–64).

The key to the Court's holding that the school acted within its rights, and also the key distinction from *Tinker*, was that the school newspaper was clearly a school-sponsored publication and part of the curriculum. The Court noted that an important distinction must be made between a school's ability to "silence a student's personal expression that happens to occur on the school premises," as was the case in *Tinker*, and a school's authority over school-sponsored activities that students, parents, and the community might reasonably understand to bear the imprimatur of the school, as in the current case. Such activities may be considered part of the curriculum, regardless of whether they occur in the classroom, if they are supervised by faculty members and are designed to teach students particular knowledge or skills. Educators must be able to exercise greater control over such activities for the purpose of ensuring that students learn the lessons being taught, that audiences are not exposed to material that may be inappropriate for their maturity level, and that the views expressed are not erroneously attributed to the school (*Id.* at 270–71).

Morse v. Frederick, 551 U.S. 393 (2007): Schools May Restrict Speech Reasonably Regarded as Encouraging Illegal Drug Use

Where a student was punished for displaying, at a school-sponsored event, a banner that the principal interpreted as promoting drug use, the Supreme Court held that schools may take steps to safeguard those entrusted to their care from speech that can reasonably be regarded as encouraging illegal drug use (*Morse v. Frederick,* 551 U.S. 393 (2007)).

When the 2002 Olympic Torch Relay ran through town during school hours, the high school principal decided to allow the students to leave class to watch the event. Just as the runners passed by the students, a handful of students unfurled a 14-foot banner reading "BONG HiTS 4 JESUS," which was easily viewed by students on the opposite side of the street. The principal immediately demanded that the boys take down the banner. All but one complied. The principal confiscated the banner, which she thought encouraged the use of marijuana, and suspended the one student who had refused to obey her order to take it down. The student, Frederick, sued, arguing that his First Amendment rights had been infringed (*Id.* at 397–98).

Frederick claimed that the message on the banner was meaningless "gibberish" and that he had displayed it only for the purpose of attracting attention and getting on television. The Court, however, found that, regardless of Frederick's intentions or motives, it was reasonable for the principal to interpret the message as promoting the use of marijuana. School board policy expressly forbad "public expression that ... advocates the use of substances that are illegal to minors," and also established that students participating in "approved social events and class trips" were ruled by the same student conduct rules that applied in the classroom. The Court considered the event to be school-sponsored based on several factors: it occurred during school hours and was sanctioned by the principal as an official school event, teachers supervised the students in attendance, and the high school band and cheerleaders performed at the event (*Id.* at 400–402). The Court went on to expound on the prevalence of the nationwide problem of drug use amongst students, referring to some of the cases addressing student claims of violation of their constitutional rights in the context of schools enforcing antidrug policies, and held that Frederick's constitutional rights had not been violated:

> The "special characteristics of the school environment," and the governmental interest in stopping student drug abuse—reflected in the policies of Congress and myriad school boards, including JDHS—allow schools to restrict student expression that they reasonably regard as promoting illegal drug use (*Id.* at 408 [citations omitted]).

The Intersection of First Amendment Rights and Privacy

Americans tend to identify their culture strongly with First Amendment rights. Increasingly, we see the emergence of a feeling that individual privacy is a right closely associated with being an American. Ironically, however, although we as a society tend to view these two types of protections as fundamental rights of being "American," the protections act as a double-edged sword. At times, they strengthen and support each other. At other times, they contradict or conflict with each other.

For example, where a media outlet might consider reporting the identity and sexual history of a young woman accusing an internationally famous athlete of rape to be its right protected by the First Amendment, the young woman doubtless would consider the publication of such information to be an extreme invasion of her privacy that could have tremendous negative effects on her life. (See, e.g., *People v. Bryant*, 94 P.3d 624, 627 (Colo. 2004).) Similarly, where an argument can be made that a student blogger's ability to post photos of school administrators engaged in disparaging activities in their private lives is protected by the First Amendment, those administrators may also argue that the publication of such photos invades their privacy and could have tremendous negative effects on their lives.

In such cases, when the right of speech collides with the right of privacy, which rights should prevail? How should we decide?

Perhaps the perfect storm of the intersection of First Amendment rights and privacy rights can be found in the context of anonymous and pseudonymous speech.

The Supreme Court has held that a speaker's right to remain anonymous is protected by the First Amendment (*McIntyre v. Ohio Elections Comm'n*, 514 U.S. 334, 342 (1995)). And yet, here we clearly see the double-edged sword. Whereas a great deal might never be expressed without the protection of anonymity, anonymity has also been used throughout time as a weapon for various sorts of harassment. The very anonymity that protects my privacy allows me to invade yours with a greatly reduced likelihood of being caught. On the one hand is the role of whistleblower Deep Throat in the Watergate scandal. We learned 30 years later that Deep Throat was, at the time, deputy director of the FBI. Without the protection of speaking anonymously, Deep Throat likely never would have come forward, and the extent of one of the greatest abuses of power our country has experienced may never have been known. On the other is the tragic case of Megan Meier, a young teenager whose online harassment by a schoolmate's mother, using a pseudonym, led to Megan's suicide.

Anonymity and pseudonymity, of course, are made much simpler and easier in the Internet environment and may be particularly attractive to minors, for whom role-playing is a part of life. For children, and perhaps even more so teenagers and traditional-aged college students, who are trying out different personas, investigating who they are, and testing out who they might become, the ability to interact with others anonymously or pseudonymously can be like opening the gates to a limitless world—they can literally be anyone they want to be. (See Kumayama 2009.) While this ability can help them define themselves by giving them a safe environment for experimentation, it can also have negative and even dire repercussions. The same sense of security can both encourage young people to abuse others and make them targets for abuse themselves.

We also see the intersection of free speech and privacy rights when a lack of privacy protections results in a chilling effect on speech. Much has been written, and many studies conducted, on the chilling effect created by surveillance. When we know we are being watched, we simply behave differently; we modify our behavior to escape negative repercussions from the observer or to increase the likelihood of receiving positive repercussions. In some cases, the suspicion of being watched can affect behavior more dramatically than knowing we are being watched. (See, e.g., Kang 1998; Kumayama 2009.) One cannot help but think of George Orwell's *1984*. If we know, or suspect, that our speech is being monitored, we do not feel free to express ourselves as we might otherwise.

The Supreme Court has made clear that the First Amendment protection of expression includes the right to receive information. (See, e.g., *Board of Educ., Island Trees Union Free Sch. Dist. v. Pico*, 457 U.S. 853 (1982).) This right may be infringed upon when the privacy of certain information is not protected. A prime example is the need to protect the records of library users; the lack of protection for library usage records can have a chilling effect on what users choose to research or read, thus discouraging them from exercising their First Amendment rights. A commonly used example is that of a sexually active teenager seeking information about birth control or protection from sexually transmitted disease. The teen may fear repercussion from parents or other adults should they learn of her sexual activity. If she believes that her parents can easily obtain records of her Internet searches and books checked out of a library, she is likely to avoid researching these issues that are very important to her health. For this reason, most libraries have a policy of keeping private and regularly purging individually identifiable usage information, and, thanks to the advocacy of librarians, most states also have laws protecting library records.

Furthermore, considering the important role played by educational institutions of all levels in making good citizens out of their students, as articulated by the Supreme Court in more than one decision (see, e.g., *Bethel Sch. Dist. No. 403 v. Fraser*, 478 U.S. 675 (1986)), it is particularly incumbent on education officials to attempt to ensure that institutional policies and procedures do not invade the privacy rights of students—be they young children or middle-aged college students—such that students would feel restricted in the ability to exercise First Amendment rights of freedom of expression, speech, and association. To do so would be to create a chilling effect on the educational environment.

BIBLIOGRAPHY

Bethel Sch. Dist. No. 403 v. Fraser, 478 U.S. 675 (1986).

Board of Educ., Island Trees Union Free Sch. Dist. v. Pico, 457 U.S. 853 (1982).

Draper v. United States, 358 U.S. 307 (1959).

Farber, Daniel A., *The First Amendment*, 2nd ed. (New York: Foundation Press, 2003).

Fewless v. Board of Educ., 208 F. Supp. 2d 806, 813 (W.D. Mich. 2002).

Hazelwood Sch. Dist. v. Kuhlmeier, 484 U.S. 260 (1988).

Jameson, Sarah, "Cyberharassment: Striking a Balance Between Free Speech and Privacy," 17 *CommLaw Conspectus* 231 (2008).

Kang, Jerry, "Information Privacy in Cyberspace Transactions," 50 *Stan. L. Rev.* 1193 (1998).

Katz v. United States, 389 U.S. 347 (1967).

Kumayama, Ken D., "A Right to Pseudonymity," 51 *Ariz. L. Rev.* 427 (2009).

McIntyre v. Ohio Elections Comm'n, 514 U.S. 334 (1995).

Michigan v. Chesternut, 486 U.S. 567 (1988).

M.J. v. State of Florida, 399 So. 2d 996 (1981).

Morse v. Frederick, 551 U.S. 393 (2007).

New Jersey v. T.L.O., 469 U.S. 325 (1985).

People v. Bryant, 94 P.3d 624 (Colo. 2004).

Rapp, James, *Education Law* (New York: Matthew Bender & Co., 2012).

Rubin v. Coors Brewing Co., 514 U.S. 476 (1995).

Schenck v. United States, 249 U.S. 47 (1919).

Tinker v. Des Moines Indep. Cmty. Sch. Dist., 393 U.S. 503 (1969).

Liability under the Law

The preceding chapters have explored the laws protecting privacy in the educational environment, but what are the consequences of violating those laws? Not surprisingly, given the piecemeal approach of U.S. privacy law, the answer depends on what type of right is being violated and which law or laws apply.

It is worth noting here that, regardless of the type of claim filed, a lawsuit is usually a long, expensive, and emotionally draining process. Furthermore, in some cases, financial damages are not available for infringement of privacy rights, leaving a plaintiff with no ability to recoup the expenses of a lawsuit. Thus, it is safe to say that the majority of violations never result in lawsuits. Some commentators argue that the legal system should be reformed to make it easier for victims of privacy infringement to pursue legal action. (See, e.g., Connallon 2007; Graw Leary 2011; Sanchez Abril 2007.)

Of course, in addition to the expensive and often arduous process of suing, many other reasons exist to seek alternative remedies. The parties should consider what their goals and desired outcomes are. Perhaps the top priority is to clarify or amend the school's policy and procedures, and to ensure that all employees understand how to appropriately apply the policy. In such case, a combination of mediation and educational activities might be the most beneficial path.

Despite what might appear to be a clear demarcation as described in this chapter, determining what type of claim applies to a particular situation is dependent on the details of the situation and can become quite complicated. For example, even if the right violated is a constitutional right, if a statute applies to the particular act at issue, the claim may have to be brought under that statute and not as infringement of a constitutional right.

Most statutes addressing specific situations, such as those discussed in Chapter 2, will include their own specific enforcement and liability provisions. This chapter will address the broader areas of liability for torts and constitutional violations.

In the educational context, claims of violation of privacy rights are usually brought under one of two broad areas of law: violation of either a constitutional right or a tort. Note that, because the Constitution applies only to governmental entities, a private institution and its officials and employees cannot be held liable for violation of constitutional rights. They may, however, be liable under tort law.

While it is possible that they may either result in or be associated with a criminal act, violations of privacy likely to occur in the educational context are not in and of themselves criminal in nature. For example, entering someone's home without their authorization to search for particular items may constitute both civil (i.e., noncriminal) infringement of privacy rights as well as the criminal act of breaking and entering. Likewise, hacking into a school's network could involve the criminal act of breaking into a secure system as well as civil law invasions of privacy by accessing protected data.

Because the rights violated are personal and not criminal in nature, claims—legal action—must be brought by the alleged victim (or, in the case of minors, the parents would bring suit on behalf of the minor).

TORT

A tort is a "private or civil wrong or injury . . . for which the court will provide a remedy in the form of an action for damages. . . . There must always be a violation of some duty owing to plaintiff, and generally such duty must arise by operation of law . . ." (Black 1991, 1036). The remedy offered by a suit in tort is financial damages.

Who May Be Held Liable

Depending on the circumstances, both the individuals engaged in the violations and the institution may be held liable. Assuming immunity does not apply, as discussed below, the entity may be held liable under one of two theories. If the individual actor is an official, officer, or decision-maker of the institution, the institution or governing board may be held directly liable, because the individual is acting on behalf of the institution. If the violation occurs as the result of an employee acting within the scope of his or her employment, the doctrine of vicarious, or imputed, liability may hold the institution, but not a governing board, liable (Rapp 2012, §1206). An employee acts within the scope of his or her employment if the act is of the type he or she is hired to perform; it occurs mostly within the time and space authorized by the employer; it is undertaken, at least in part, by a purpose to perform his or her duties; and, if force is used against someone else, the force is not unexpectable by the employer. Even if not authorized by the employer, the conduct may be found to be within the scope of employment if it is so similar or incidental to authorized conduct that it would fit into the scope of employment (Restatement (Second) of Agency 1958, §228). Several factors are to be considered in determining whether an act unauthorized by an employer could nevertheless be considered to fall within the scope of employment, including whether it is an act commonly undertaken by employees, whether or not the employer had reason to expect that such act would be undertaken, similarity in quality to authorized acts, and the extent to which the act departs from the normal method of accomplishing an authorized result (*Id.* §229).

Remedies

Because tort law is a matter of state law, details of remedies available will differ from state to state. At the minimum, compensation for actual harm caused will be available; the plaintiff will usually have to prove the harm and that it was directly caused by the defendant's acts. Many state tort laws allow for damages for emotional distress, mental anguish, and the like. Some states will also provide punitive damages, usually only in egregious situations. Simply put: The remedies available to a plaintiff who prevails in a tort action of violation of privacy rights are different in each state.

VIOLATION OF CONSTITUTIONAL RIGHT

Although the prohibitions against infringement of citizens' rights in the Bill of Rights as originally written applied only to the federal government, the Fourteenth Amendment expanded those prohibitions to actions by state governments, and the Civil Action for Deprivation of Rights Act ("Section 1983"), passed shortly thereafter, established a cause of action in the courts for violations of those rights (42 U.S.C. §1983). Both were passed in the aftermath of the Civil War. More recently, the Supreme Court has made clear that Section 1983 was intended to provide a remedy to private citizens for violations of their rights granted by the Constitution and federal law by those acting under the authority of state law (*Monroe v. Pape*, 365 U.S. 167 (1961); *Mitchum v. Foster*, 407 U.S. 225 (1972)). The Court has also made clear that public school boards and school officials are considered to be representatives of the state for such purposes (*New Jersey v. T.L.O.*, 469 U.S. 325, 336 (1985)).

Who May Be Held Liable

As with torts, in addition to the individual engaged in the infringing action, the institution and/or the individual's supervisor may be held liable for the violation under certain circumstances.

An institution may be found liable under Section 1983 (that is, liable for infringement of constitutional rights) when all of the following conditions are met:

1. The infringement of a constitutional right is a result of the individual acting in line with either the institution's stated policy or custom, that is, the individual's action reflects a standard practice in responding to the type of situation at issue. (See, e.g., *Springfield v. Kibbe*, 480 U.S. 257, 267 (1987).)

2. The allegedly infringing act is the actual cause of the infringement of the plaintiff's constitutional right. (See, e.g., *City of Canton v. Harris*, 489 U.S. 378, 385 (1989).)

3. The individual actor has the authority to make final decisions for the institution in the type of situation at issue. In determining whether the individual has this level of authority, a court must take into consideration "relevant legal materials," such as state and local law, as well as institutional customs. (See, e.g., *Jett v. Dallas Indep. Sch. Dist.*, 491 U.S. 701, 737 (1989).)

An individual supervisor may be held liable for a subordinate's infringement of another's constitutional rights if any one of the following apply:

1. the supervisor participated directly in the alleged constitutional violation,

2. the supervisor, after being informed of the violation, failed to remedy the wrong,

3. the supervisor created a policy or custom under which unconstitutional practices occurred, or allowed the continuance of such a policy or custom,

4. the supervisor was grossly negligent in supervising subordinates who committed the wrongful acts, or

5. the supervisor exhibited deliberate indifference to the rights of others by failing to act on information indicating that unconstitutional acts were occurring (*Johnson v. Newburgh Enlarged Sch. Dist.*, 239 F.3d 246, 254 (2d Cir. 2001)).

Immunity

Under the Eleventh Amendment, state governments themselves are immune from Section 1983 liability. However, determining whether immunity extends to an extension of the state, such as a school district or college or university system, depends on several factors. The Ninth Circuit has succinctly articulated these factors as, based on the way state law treats the entity, "whether a money judgment would be satisfied out of state funds, whether the entity performs central governmental functions, whether the entity may sue or be sued, whether the entity has the power to take property in its own name or only the name of the state, and the corporate status of the entity" (*Mitchell v. Los Angeles Cmty. Coll. Dist.*, 861 F.2d 198, 201 (9th Cir. 1988)). Because the determination is so fact-specific, educational entities of all sorts —governing boards, district and system administrations, and schools—have been granted immunity in some cases and denied immunity in others. In addition, where immunity does apply, it may extend to protect state officials sued in their official capacity (as opposed to being sued in their capacity as individuals not representing the institution) (Rapp 2012, §12.03).

Officials of the state are given "qualified immunity," meaning that they are immune from liability when they have a good faith belief, based on reasonable grounds, that their actions, taken in their official capacity, did not infringe the rights alleged to have been violated. This determination is based on a totality of the circumstances at the time the alleged violation occurred. This immunity has been extended to almost all levels of educational personnel, at all levels of public education (*Id.*). Qualified immunity will not be granted where the official knew or reasonably should have known that his or her actions would violate constitutional rights or where the action was undertaken with malicious intent to violate such rights or cause other injury to the victim (*Wood v. Strickland*, 420 U.S. 308 (1975)).

Remedies

Financial damages, attorneys' fees, injunctive relief, and generally any other type of relief a court believes may be necessary to remedy the wrongs done may be awarded in a suit under Section 1983 (Rapp 2012, §12.03). For monetary damages compensating the plaintiff to be awarded, the plaintiff must prove that the violation of his or her rights caused actual damage for which he or she can be compensated. In addition, punitive damages may be awarded only against defendants sued in their capacity as individuals; they will not be awarded against an institution or a defendant sued in his or her official capacity. Attorneys' fees may also be awarded (*Id.*).

When the government violates someone's Fourth Amendment rights in the criminal context, which is where Fourth Amendment claims most often arise, the remedy will be to suppress any evidence obtained due to the violation.

BIBLIOGRAPHY

American Library Association, "Privacy: An Interpretation of the Library Bill of Rights," http://www.ala.org/advocacy/intfreedom/librarybill/interpretations/accessdigital (July 6, 2013).

Black's Law Dictionary, 6th ed. (St. Paul, MN: West Group, 1991).

City of Canton v. Harris, 489 U.S. 378 (1989).

Connallon, Robert M., "An Integrative Alternative for America's Privacy Torts," 38 *Golden Gate U.L. Rev.* 71 (2007).

Graw Leary, Mary, "Reasonable Expectations of Privacy for Youth in a Digital Age," 80 *Miss. L.J.* 1033 (2011).

Jett v. Dallas Indep. Sch. Dist., 491 U.S. 701 (1989).

Johnson v. Newburgh Enlarged Sch. Dist., 239 F.3d 246 (2d Cir. 2001).

Mitchell v. Los Angeles Cmty. Coll. Dist., 861 F.2d 198 (9th Cir. 1988).

Mitchum v. Foster, 407 U.S. 225 (1972).

Monroe v. Pape, 365 U.S. 167 (1961).

New Jersey v. T.L.O., 469 U.S. 325, 336 (1985).

Rapp, James, *Education Law* (New York: Matthew Bender & Co. 2012).

Restatement (Second) of Agency (St. Paul, MN: West Publishing Co., 1958).

Sanchez Abril, Patricia, "Recasting Privacy Torts in a Spaceless World," 21 *Harv. J. Law & Tec* 1 (2007).

Springfield v. Kibbe, 480 U.S. 257 (1987).

Thro, William E., "The Education Lawyer's Guide to the Sovereign Immunity Revolution," 146 *Educ. L. R.* 951 (2000).

Wood v. Strickland, 420 U.S. 308 (1975).

PART II

Applications in the Educational Setting

Understanding how any area of law applies in the educational setting is made easier by understanding how the law—including the courts—views the relationship between educational institutions and students. The nature of that relationship varies depending, in part, on the level of student, whether the school is publicly or privately funded, and the type of activity involved. For example, the relationship between institution and student in the K–12 setting is approached in a different way than in the higher education setting. Similarly, it is viewed differently in a classroom setting than in the context of extracurricular activities. Furthermore, the view of this relationship changes over time, as our societal goals for education change, reflecting evolution of our social values (Rapp 2012, §8.01).

Defining the nature of the relationship is important because it defines the responsibility of the educational institution. Is the school responsible for providing a safe and healthy learning environment? Most educators, students, and parents would probably say yes, it is. But to what extent? And to what extent would or should this responsibility differ between different levels of institutions? While it may be clear that a school should respond to existing or foreseeable problems, to what extent must it act to prevent problems from occurring? Consider as an example the possession of weapons in schools. Few would argue in support of students having a right to bring weapons onto campus. Setting aside the question of what constitutes a weapon (consider the six-year-old boy who faced a 45-day suspension for bringing to school a Boy Scout camping utensil that served as spoon, fork, and knife [Urbina 2009]), to what extent does an educational institution have a responsibility to prevent students from bringing weapons onto the property? Most importantly for our purposes: How does that responsibility intersect with a student's right to privacy?

Traditionally in the United States, both K–12 and postsecondary schools have been considered to act as *in loco parentis*, or "in place of the parent," meaning with the authority and responsibility to act as a parent in the parent's absence. For many years, this meant that educators were given almost unfettered authority in their interactions with students. During the twentieth century, as social values generally tended to move towards an increasing recognition of individual rights, the rights of minors also became an issue. For decades, the Supreme Court has recognized the constitutional rights of minors, perhaps most famously in a First Amendment case in which the Court stated, "It can hardly be argued that either students or teachers shed their constitutional rights to freedom of speech or expression at the schoolhouse gate" (*Tinker v. Des Moines Indep. Cmty. Sch. Dist.*, 393 U.S. 503, 507 (1969)). In this context, the *in loco parentis* doctrine has been greatly tempered by balancing its application with the growing recognition of the rights of students. The Supreme Court has repeatedly referred to this balancing act, stating in 1985 that the suggestion that an educational institution should have the same authority as a parent is "in tension with contemporary reality" and that "Today's public school officials do not merely exercise authority voluntarily conferred on them by individual parents; rather, they act in furtherance of publicly mandated educational and disciplinary policies" (*New Jersey v. T.L.O.*, 469 U.S. 325, 336 (1985)). The Court rejected the *in loco parentis* doctrine as no longer appropriate in modern society and clarified that school officials act as representatives of the state, not of parents, when they engage in disciplinary functions (*Id.*).

The Court has also long recognized that, in this role, primary and secondary school officials have a unique duty to protect our children, both physically and otherwise. (See, e.g., *Shelton v. Tucker*, 364 U.S. 479, 487 (1960); *West Virginia State Bd. of Ed. v. Barnette*, 319 U.S. 624, 637 (1943).) Although public attention to the problem of unsafe schools exploded in the 1970s, along with increasing acknowledgement of the problem by officials at all levels, from Congress to local school boards, no law creates a broad right to a safe educational environment for students or faculty and staff. California's attempt to implement legislation that would do so provides an example of how tricky this can be. In 1978, California voters passed an amendment to the state's constitution referred to as the "Victim's Bill of Rights," which was part of a comprehensive package of reforms to the criminal justice system and included the statement: "All Students and Staff of public primary, elementary, junior high and senior high schools have the inalienable right to attend campuses that are safe, secure and peaceful" (Cal. Const. art. I, § 28(c)). Although application of this enunciated right has proved elusive, passage of the bill has increased attention to the issue, including encouraging California's courts to extend special deference to school attempts to ensure safety (Rapp 2012, §9.01). This is, of course, only an example; not all states have gone down the road of extending a benefit of the doubt to educational institutions in such situations.

The federal No Child Left Behind Act includes what is known as the "Unsafe School Choice Option," in which states receiving funds under the Elementary and Secondary Education Act are required to establish a statewide policy giving the option for students who attend "persistently dangerous" schools, or who become victim of a violent criminal offense while on the grounds of a public school, to be transferred to a safe school within the same district (20 U.S.C. §7912). The act does not apply to public institutions of higher education.

Of course, laws not specific to the educational context address many situations creating safety issues, such as laws that prohibit the use or sale of certain drugs and laws prohibiting the possession of guns on campuses. These laws differ from state to state. Institutional policies also typically address these and other safety concerns.

Regardless of law or lack thereof, educational institutions do feel a duty to provide a safe and secure learning environment for their students, and their communities expect it of them. But what rights must be traded off in order to create this security? The discussion in Chapter 2 of the USA PATRIOT Act noted the trade-off necessary to establish national security: by necessity, we as a society surrender some degree of privacy rights we would otherwise have in order to increase the degree of safety we feel. For example, in exchange for feeling safer flying, we deem it acceptable to surrender some level of privacy in our persons (when we walk through a scanner at the airport gate) and our things (when we open our checked bags to find the note card informing us that TSA agents have searched them). Challenges arise in attempting to draw the lines, to decide how much we want to give up of one right in order to get more of the other. In the context of airport security, most airline travelers are perfectly willing to walk through a metal detector and have their shoes and personal baggage x-rayed, but they differ, sometimes vehemently, in which they feel is more invasive of their privacy: body scanners or physical pat-downs. How do we balance safety in educational institutions with other rights of minor students, adult students, faculty, and staff, specifically privacy rights?

As technology evolves, we are faced with a seemingly endless string of choices in this context, as implied in the example above of differing opinions regarding airport security methods. While technology provides us with wonderful opportunities for growth and development, it can also become a tool for damage. The use of ever-evolving technology for security in airports is partly a response to the use of ever-evolving technology by terrorists. Likewise, as digital technology evolves, it offers us an entirely new world of possibilities in the educational environment for teaching and learning, interacting with others, and reaching across cultural and language barriers. It also introduces new possibilities for hurting others, from simple embarrassment to cyberbullying to online child predation. And in response, it offers us increasing abilities to fight against such abuses by monitoring the online activities of our students and employees. But where do we draw the lines? To what extent do we deem it acceptable to invade the privacy rights of others for the sake of security?

Chapters 5 and 6 address student privacy rights. Chapter 5 will discuss how established law addresses these questions in the context of creating a safe educational environment in the physical world. Chapter 6 will discuss the challenges of attempting to apply these laws to an ever-changing technological world. The latter is no easy task in a world in which the development of technology seems to accelerate every day; in which we as a society struggle to understand how our changing use of technology affects our social norms and values; and in which the development of law merely trudges along. Chapter 7 will address how the privacy rights of faculty and staff may be implicated in efforts to create a safe educational environment.

BIBLIOGRAPHY

New Jersey v. T.L.O., *469 U.S.* 325 (1985).

Rapp, James, *Education Law* (New York: Matthew Bender & Co. 2012).

Shelton v. Tucker, 364 U.S. 479 (1960).

Tinker v. Des Moines Indep. Cmty. Sch. Dist., 393 U.S. 503 (1969).

Urbina, Ian, "It's a Fork, It's a Spoon, It's a . . . Weapon?," *New York Times*, October 9, 2009.

West Virginia State Bd. of Ed. v. Barnette, 319 U.S. 624 (1943).

CHAPTER 5

Student Privacy in the Brick-and-Mortar World

As always, keep in mind that most states have their own laws addressing some of the issues discussed in this chapter. The right of public officials to search or seize a person or his or her belongings is limited by the Fourth Amendment:

> The right of the people to be secure in their persons, houses, papers, and effects, against unreasonable searches and seizures, shall not be violated, and no Warrants shall issue, but upon probable cause, supported by Oath or affirmation, and particularly describing the place to be searched, and the persons or things to be seized (U.S. Const. amend. IV).

The key is defining what constitutes an "unreasonable" search or seizure. As discussed in Chapter 3, a search or seizure will always be reasonable if conducted under the auspices of a warrant. However, the courts have recognized that in many situations, obtaining a warrant is impractical and thus contrary to the public interest being served by the public officials. The educational context is one of those. This chapter will discuss how that determination has been made in a variety of situations in the educational setting.

Although Fourth Amendment restrictions do not apply to private institutions, many state constitutions and tort laws prohibiting an invasion of privacy are based on the concepts and standards that have developed under Fourth Amendment law. Thus, the following discussion should be valuable to private institutions as they consider what policy is appropriate for their own situation. As always, though, because each institution and each situation is different, you should consult your institution's legal counsel as appropriate.

REASONABLE SEARCHES IN THE EDUCATIONAL CONTEXT

Students Have a Reasonable Expectation of Privacy

As discussed in Chapter 3, to constitute an unreasonable search, the search must intrude on a person's reasonable expectation of privacy. Another way to state this is: No right to privacy can exist if no reasonable expectation of privacy exists.

The Supreme Court has held several times that students in the educational setting, regardless of age, have a reasonable expectation of privacy in their persons and belongings. However, that expectation is limited due to the "tension" between the student's right of privacy and "the interest of the States in providing a safe environment conducive to education in the public schools" (*New Jersey v. T.L.O.*, 469 U.S. 325, 332 n.2 (1985)). Nonetheless, the Court has said that the belief that "because of the pervasive supervision to which children in the schools are necessarily subject, a child has virtually no legitimate expectation of privacy in articles of personal property 'unnecessarily' carried into a school" is "severely flawed" (*Id.* at 338 [citations omitted]).

The question, then, is: Given that primary and secondary students have a reasonable but limited expectation of privacy for themselves and their belongings while on school property, how do we determine what constitutes a reasonable search or seizure in the K–12 school context? And since students of higher education are subject to much less "pervasive supervision" than younger students, what constitutions a reasonable search or seizure in the higher education context?

The Standard

The standard to be used in determining the constitutionality of a search of students or their possessions in an educational setting has been labeled simply "reasonableness." Reasonableness is determined based on the entirety of the circumstances. To be reasonable, the search must be (1) justified at its inception and (2) reasonably related in scope to the circumstances that justified the search (*New Jersey v. T.L.O.*, 469 U.S. 325, 341 (1985)).

The case setting this standard is *New Jersey v. T.L.O.*, decided by the Supreme Court in 1985. Although the facts of the case involved a secondary school student, the standard set by the Court is applicable in all educational institutions subject to the Fourth Amendment (that is, those that are public institutions). In this case, T.L.O. was a female high school freshman whom a teacher discovered in a restroom with another student who herself was smoking. The teacher took the girls to the assistant vice principal. Although her friend admitted to smoking in violation of a school policy, T.L.O. claimed that she had not been smoking and that she did not smoke at all. The vice principal took her to his private office, where he opened her purse and found a pack of cigarettes and also noticed a pack of rolling papers. Because the rolling papers made him suspect that T.L.O. smoked marijuana, he thoroughly searched her purse. His search revealed marijuana, a pipe, empty plastic bags, a large number of one-dollar bills, an index card with a list of students who owed money to T.L.O., and two letters implicating her in dealing marijuana. The vice principal notified her mother as well as the police and gave the evidence to the police. T.L.O. later confessed to the police that she had been selling marijuana. In response to charges brought against her in juvenile court, she moved to suppress the evidence found in her purse as well as her confession. The case made its way to the Supreme Court, which confirmed that public school students do have Fourth Amendment rights and held that the search of T.L.O.'s purse did not violate these rights (*Id.*).

The Court began by emphasizing its multiple holdings over time that the Fourth Amendment limitations on searches and seizures applies not only to law enforcement but to civil as well as criminal authorities, including building inspectors, Occupational Safety and Health Act inspectors, and firefighters. School officials are acting in their capacity as representatives of the state and are thus subject to Fourth Amendment limitations. Further, based on established Supreme Court jurisprudence, a reasonable expectation of privacy exists for the owner of any container concealing its contents from closed view, including those of children (*Id.* at 335). Thus, T.L.O. had a reasonable expectation of privacy in her purse, and the school was required to abide by the Fourth Amendment limitations in searching it (*Id.*).

The Court went on to discuss the challenges of balancing the "substantial" interest of the school to maintain discipline in the learning environment with the privacy rights of students, noting that doing so "requires [application of] a certain degree of flexibility in school disciplinary proceedings" (*Id.* at 340).

The Court labeled as simply "reasonableness" the standard to be used to meet Fourth Amendment protections in searches of students and their belongings the school context. The reasonableness of a search is determined based on (1) whether the search was justified at its inception and (2) whether the scope of the search as conducted was reasonable in the context of the circumstances that justified it in the first place.

Under ordinary circumstances, a search of a student by an institution's official will be will be "justified at its inception" when there are reasonable grounds for suspecting that the search will turn up evidence that the student has violated or is violating either the law or the rules of the institution. Such a search will be permissible in its scope when the measures adopted are reasonably related to the objectives of the search and not excessively intrusive in light of the age and sex of the student and the nature of the infraction (*Id.* at 341–42).

This standard, the Court stated, meets the Fourth Amendment requirement to ensure that searches are reasonable by finding the balance between ensuring that students' rights will be invaded no more than necessary while also providing the institution's officials with the ability to "regulate [student] conduct according to the dictates of reason and common sense" (*Id.* at 343).

The Court differentiated between two searches conducted by the principal: the first, for cigarettes, and the second, for marijuana. Because the second flowed from results of the first, if the first was unconstitutional, the second would be as well. This follows from application of the "poisonous fruits" doctrine, which mandates that any proceeds flowing from an unconstitutional search are contaminated and must also be treated as unconstitutionally obtained. The Court found the act of searching the purse to be reasonable, because, although not certain proof that she had been smoking, finding cigarettes in T.L.O.'s possession would at least corroborate the accusation of smoking as well as undermine her credibility in denying she had been smoking. Given these circumstances, the vice principal needed only a "reasonable suspicion" that T.L.O.'s purse contained cigarettes. When he picked up the cigarettes, the vice principal spotted the rolling papers. It was thus reasonable for him to further search her purse for evidence of marijuana. Thus, both searches were justified at inception (*Id.* at 344–45).

Regarding the scope of the searches, T.L.O.'s primary complaint was that the vice principal infringed her rights by reading the letters that implicated her in drug dealing. The Court held that, given the multiple pieces of evidence found in T.L.O.'s purse, it was reasonable for the vice principal to extend the search to reading the letters to determine if they contained additional evidence (*Id.* at 347).

The *T.L.O.* Court emphasized that its holding applied only to the situation in front of it and did not extend to the expectation of privacy regarding possessions not in the student's control, such as lockers, desks, or other school property (*Id.* at 338).

"Individualized" versus "Generalized" Searches

In applying the reasonableness standard articulated in *T.L.O.*, a court will consider whether the official's suspicion is "individualized," meaning directed at an individual student (or sometimes an identified group of students), as opposed to a "generalized" suspicion, meaning a suspicion that someone somewhere within a body of students may be engaged in illicit activity. For example, an individualized suspicion would be a reasonable suspicion that Jane Johns is carrying a weapon. A generalized suspicion would be a reasonable suspicion that some students in the school, whose identities are unknown, may be carrying weapons.

Generally, a search in response to individualized suspicion is more likely to be considered reasonable; when searches are conducted in response to generalized suspicions, courts are more likely to set a higher standard for the educational institution, requiring the existence of exigent circumstances in order to find the search reasonable.

An Eighth Circuit case provides a good example. The Little Rock School District had a practice, supported by its written policies, of at random times and without notice requiring students to empty their pockets and set all of their belongings, including book bags, purses, and wallets, on their desks, and then leave the classroom. This is an example of a "generalized" search (also called an "administrative" or "suspicionless" search). While the students waited in the hallway, school personnel searched their belongings. If illegal items such as drugs or weapons were discovered, the school turned them over to the police. The Eighth Circuit found that these searches were unconstitutional and violated the students' privacy rights (*Doe v. Little Rock Sch. Dist.*, 380 F.3d 349, 356–57 (8th Cir. 2004)).

The court began by noting Supreme Court holdings that students do have a right to privacy, albeit limited, in the personal items they bring to school. It went on to emphasize that an institution cannot eliminate this right by claiming in its handbook that the right does not exist (*Id.* at 354). (See above for further discussion.)

Balancing the nature of the searches, the purpose served, and the nature and immediacy of the official's concerns, the court held the searches to be unreasonable.

In considering the nature of the searches, the court found them highly intrusive, based in part on the generalized, suspicionless nature, and in part on the extremely personal nature of the items thoroughly searched. The student's privacy rights, the court stated, were "wholly obliterated" by the practice of searching belongings of a very personal nature "at any time without notice, individualized suspicion, or any apparent limit to the extensiveness of the search" (*Id.* at 355). In addressing the objectives served by the searches, the court pointed out that by turning over all evidence of illegal activity to the police, the district was "playing a law enforcement role," implying that the higher standard of probable cause should apply (*Id.*). The court turned finally to the nature and immediacy of the official's concerns. The district claimed that the searches were necessary to prevent students from bringing drugs and weapons onto the campus. However, the district could not point to any evidence indicating it had experienced "significant and immediate difficulties sufficient to give right" to such an intrusive method of searching (*Id.* at 356).

This case provides an excellent example of how a court balances the intrusiveness of a search with the level of harm the institution seeks to prevent, including how immediate the threat is. That the searches were random, generalized, and suspicionless contributed to the degree of invasiveness. "All schools surely have an interest in minimizing the harm that the existence of weapons and controlled substances might visit upon a student population, but public schools have never been entitled to conduct random, full-scale searches of students' personal belongings because of a mere apprehension" (*Id.*).

Generalized searches may be reasonable under other circumstances. The *Doe* Court compared the situation before it to that of a case in which it had "upheld a blanket school search somewhat like the one at issue here when school officials had received specific information giving them reasonable grounds to believe that the students' safety was in jeopardy" (*Id.*). In *Thompson v. Carthage School District*, the principal of a very small school that encompassed grades one through twelve was told by a bus driver that he had found fresh cuts on some bus seats. The principal was concerned that a student had brought a knife to school and so instituted a search of all boys from sixth through twelfth grades. The students were brought into a room, where they were told to empty their pockets and to take off their jackets, shoes, and socks. Those items were placed on a table and searched. The students were searched with a metal detector; if the detector indicated the presence of metal, the student was then given a pat-down. At some point during the search process, some students told the principal that a gun had been seen at school that morning. The lawsuit was brought by a student who was found to have crack cocaine in his jacket pocket. The court held the search to be "generalized but minimally intrusive"; given that the principal was searching for dangerous weapons for which she had "two independent reasons to suspect ... had been brought to school that morning," the search was reasonable (*Thompson v. Carthage Sch. Dist.*, 87 F.3d 979 (8th Cir. 1996)).

As with individualized searches, such as in *T.L.O.*, the more invasive a generalized search, the more threatening must be the circumstances justifying the invasion of privacy. However, generalized searches start off with the assumption that they are by nature intrusive. Thus, the Eighth Circuit has said that generalized searches will be constitutional only if there is "evidence of unique circumstances that would justify significant intrusions" (*Doe*, 380 F.3d at 356–57). Nonetheless, courts regularly find generalized searches using methods such as metal detectors to be minimally invasive and reasonable (*Id.* at 355).

Applying the Standard

The first question to be asked in any Fourth Amendment (and many tort) privacy case is whether the plaintiff had a reasonable expectation of privacy. If no reasonable expectation of privacy exists, the Constitution (or tort or other applicable law) simply is not implicated.

Once a reasonable expectation of privacy has been established, the court will proceed to consider whether the search was reasonable at its inception and then reasonable in its scope.

A search is reasonable at its inception if the student has voluntarily consented. Consent is considered voluntary if the person giving consent reasonably believes that he or she has the option to refuse. In the educational context, in analyzing whether supposed consent was actually voluntary, a court will consider factors such as the student's age, mental capacity, and education;

whether the student understands his or her rights; whether the student has been subject to any coercion or duress; and the length and nature of detention when the student is questioned. See Chapter 3 for further discussion on the issue of consent.

If voluntary consent has not been given, the court will consider the search to be reasonable at its inception if reasonable grounds exist for suspecting that the search will turn up evidence that the student has violated or is violating either the law or the rules of the institution.

The final question of whether the search is reasonable in scope attempts to balance two factors. On one hand is the official's need to maintain order and discipline. On the other is the need to protect the privacy of the student. On one side of the scale, then, we weigh whether the measures adopted for conducting the search are reasonably related to the objectives of the search, based on "nature and immediacy of the governmental concern at issue"—how serious the alleged infraction is—and the efficacy of the means employed for dealing with it (*Vernonia Sch. Dist. 47J v. Acton*, 515 U.S. 646, 654–66 (1995)). On the other hand, we weigh the nature of the invasion of privacy, which must be not excessively intrusive in light of the age and sex of the student and the nature of the infraction (*New Jersey v. T.L.O.*, 469 U.S. 325, 341–42 (1985)). Thus, for less serious infractions, searches should be minimally invasive.

SEARCHING STUDENT POSSESSIONS

Clearly, the *T.L.O.* standard will apply to searching nonelectronic student possessions, such as purses, backpacks, and packages. (Chapter 6 addresses the challenges in applying *T.L.O.* to searches of electronic items.) The scope of the search should be clearly limited by the objectives of the search. The *T.L.O.* Court found the reading of the student's letters to be reasonable based on the fact that evidence of her drug use had already been found; if the principal had found no evidence in her purse before finding the letters, and thus suspected her only of smoking cigarettes and not the more dangerous marijuana, reading the letters found in her purse likely would not have been considered reasonable.

Student Expectation of Privacy in Belongings Stored on School Property

Whether a student has a reasonable expectation of privacy in possessions he or she has stored in a locker, cabinet, desk, or other school-owned property varies with the circumstances and is determined based on institutional policy and the degree of exclusivity the student is given. Where a student maintains exclusive control over his or her locker and the institution has not given notice that it retains a right through its policies to search student lockers, a student may well have a reasonable expectation of privacy in the locker. Courts frequently cite the existence of an institution's policy reserving the right to search student lockers in finding that students have no reasonable expectation of privacy in their lockers. (See, e.g., *Zamora v. Pomeroy*, 639 F.2d 662 (10th Cir. 1981).) Courts will also refuse to find a reasonable expectation of privacy in a student's locker if the institution maintains some control over the locker, such as keeping a master key to student lockers. (See, e.g., *People v. Overton*, 229 N.E.2d 596 (N.Y. 1967); *State v. Joseph T.*, 336 S.E.2d 728 (W. Va. 1985).) The same analysis should apply to other school property in which the student stores personal belongings.

Even though a student's car itself is not the property of the educational institution, courts have consistently applied the *T.L.O.* standard to searches of students' cars parked on school property. For example, courts have upheld searches of student cars when the student was suspected of smoking and was hanging out in an area of the parking lot frequently used by smokers (*Anders v. Fort Wayne Cmty. Schs.*, 124 F. Supp. 2d 618 (N.D. Ind. 2000)) and when the student smelled of smoke after arriving at school in his car and a search of his person revealed no cigarettes (*State v. Williams*, 791 N.E.2d 608 (Ill. App. 2003)).

Searches of Student Dormitory Rooms

Note that the Fourth Amendment restrictions on searches will not apply to dormitory rooms of private schools. For living quarters in public institutions, a student clearly has a reasonable expectation of privacy. However, the courts recognize that educational institutions have many legitimate reasons to search dormitory rooms to maintain the health and safety of students (Rapp 2012,§9.08). If individualized suspicion exists, a court is most likely to apply the *T.L.O.* standard. If the institution wishes to engage in generalized searches, such as routine searches for safety inspections, the institutional policy should reflect this. In such cases, it is preferable to notify students before the searches occur. The institution should consult with its legal counsel in defining a policy for generalized searches.

However, if law enforcement officials are involved in the search, other standards may apply. See below for further discussion.

SEARCHES OF STUDENTS' PERSONS

Although some searches of a student's body may be held to be reasonable, courts clearly recognize a high expectation of privacy in the body of a minor. Thus, in such cases, the school's need for conducting the search should be clear and clearly explainable. Keep in mind that the scope of any search must be both "reasonably related to the objectives of the search" and "not excessively intrusive in light of the age and sex of the student and the nature of the infraction" (*New Jersey v. T.L.O.*, 469 U.S. 325 (1985)). The more serious or threatening the reason for the search, the more invasive a search may be to be considered reasonable. The more intrusive the search, the greater must be the potential danger of the item being sought. Note, however, that some courts or state law may require even more stringent standards.

Pat-down searches of students are considered relatively noninvasive and have been upheld in cases in which students were suspected of carrying items against institutional policy, when school property has gone missing, and when students were suspected of carrying weapons (Rapp 2012, §9.08).

Strip Searches

The term "strip search" for these purposes does not necessarily mean searching a naked body. A "strip search" in the context of an educational institution's officials searching a student refers to the removal of items of clothing or exposure of private parts of the body beneath clothing (*Id.*). The Supreme Court addressed the issue of strip searches conducted by school officials in what has become a somewhat infamous case in which a 13-year-old girl, Redding, was strip searched in an effort to find ibuprofen and naproxen hidden in her clothing. Although both drugs are typically sold over the counter, the school's policies forbad students from possessing any medications without prior permission (*Safford Unified Sch. Dist. v. Redding*, 557 U.S. 364 (2009)).

In *Redding*, a series of events occurred in which prescription-strength ibuprofen and over-the-counter naproxen had been found in the possession of at least one other student, apparently a friend of Redding, who then told the vice principal that Redding had been distributing the pills to other students. The vice principal called Redding into his office and asked if she knew anything about the pills. Redding denied any knowledge and consented to the vice principal searching her backpack and other belongings. The search uncovered no pills. The vice principal then sent the girl to the school nurse's office, where, in the presence of the nurse and an administrative aide, she was instructed to first remove her jacket, which they searched; and ultimately to strip to her underwear, pull her bra away from her body and shake it, and then pull the elastic of her underpants away from her body. No pills were uncovered (*Id.* at 368–69).

In its opinion, the Supreme Court pointed out that the vice principal's suspicion was enough to justify the searching of Redding's belongings, noting that, "If a student is reasonably suspected of giving out contraband pills, she is reasonably suspected of carrying them on her person and in [her backpack]" (*Id.* at 373). However, in applying the reasonableness standard articulated in *New Jersey v. T.L.O.* to the strip search, the Court held that "the content of the suspicion failed to match the degree of intrusion" (*Id.* at 375). The Court pointed out that the commonly used pain killers that were the subject of the search presented only a limited danger or threat, and that the vice principal had no reasonable basis to suspect that Redding was hiding painkillers in her underwear. To support a search as intrusive as this one, the Court said, there must be a reasonable suspicion either of danger or of the student using her underwear to hide evidence of an infraction (*Id.* at 376).

Although some court cases have upheld strip searches in the K–12 school setting, all were decided prior to the Supreme Court's holding in *Redding*. We have no current examples of school strip searches that have been held reasonable. The Eleventh Circuit summed up well the best approach to strip searches in a educational setting: "In fact, strip searches are probably only permissible in the school setting, if permissible at all, where there is a threat of imminent, serious harm" (*Jenkins ex rel. Hall v. Talladega City Bd. of Educ.*, 95 F.3d 1046, 1047 n.20 (11th Cir. 1996)).

Physical Examinations and Testing

Although there is little case law regarding the use of physical examinations to test students for drug and alcohol use, the case law that exists—which relies on both *T.L.O.* and Supreme Court reasoning for upholding involuntary testing in noneducational contexts—supports such testing when reasonable and individualized suspicion exists.

In a case in which a teacher had a reasonable suspicion that a student was under the influence of drugs, the Third Circuit upheld both urinalysis and blood testing. In that case, a teacher observed that high school student Tara's behavior was uncharacteristic for her, her face was flushed, her eyes were red and glassy, and her pupils dilated. He followed school policy and notified the school nurse. The nurse also concluded, based on Tara's behavior and speech, that Tara was under the influence. She tested her vital signs, some of which were slightly abnormal. Also in accordance with school policy, Tara's book bag was searched, producing a bottle containing three unidentified pills, which Tara said were diet pills. School policy prohibited students from possessing any medication without written permission and dictated that under such circumstances, the school should call the parents. Tara had trouble remembering any of her parents' phone numbers, but eventually the principal was able to contact her father. When Tara's father arrived, the principal told him that Tara would have to be tested for drug and alcohol use. The school policy stated that such an exam could be performed by a school doctor if available or by a doctor selected by the parent (at the parent's expense). The father agreed to take her to an urgent care facility, where she was given both a urinalysis and blood test. Tara later sued for, among other things, infringement of her Fourth Amendment rights (*Hedges v. Musco*, 204 F.3d 109 (3d Cir. 2000)).

The court found that, based on Tara's behavior and appearance, the suspicion of drug use was reasonable; thus, the nurse's search—taking her vital signs and observing her—was reasonable at its inception. Since the nurse's search was very limited, the scope was reasonable. The nurse's suspicion, based on her own examination of Tara, combined with the discovery of the pills in Tara's book bag, provided reasonable grounds for further searching. Since both urinalysis and blood testing are reasonable means of testing for drug use, those "searches" were reasonable at their inception (*Id.* at 117–19). The court held that the urinalysis was not excessively intrusive, as Tara gave her specimen alone in a completely private bathroom (*Id.* at 120). In considering the reasonableness of the blood test, the court noted that the Supreme Court has upheld the use of blood-alcohol tests in numerous cases, finding the method to be minimally intrusive. Thus, the court held that "requiring Tara to submit to a blood-alcohol test, administered by professionals in a medical testing clinic, was reasonable, taking into account her age, sex, and the nature of the suspected infraction" (*Id.*).

Note that the institution in this case had a detailed policy describing exactly what should happen at each step in this situation. Having such a policy in place ensures that faculty and administrators know how to respond in a given situation and also can contribute to a court's finding of reasonableness; indeed, the *Hedges* court did refer to the policy several times in its holding.

Also relevant to the court's holding in the *Hedges* case, both the teacher and the school nurse observed several specific attributes exhibited by Tara that were unusual for her and that could indicate the use of drugs, as well as finding unidentifiable pills in her bag.

In comparison, an Arkansas court found unconstitutional an involuntary urine test of students who had been in the restroom when it was filled with marijuana smoke but who otherwise exhibited no indications of marijuana possession or use. In addition, the court was concerned that the specific test used was incapable of determining when marijuana had been consumed. The combination of the inability of the test to confirm that any marijuana used had been consumed during school hours with the lack of evidence showing any kind of effect on school discipline or the students while in school led the court to hold that the testing was unconstitutional.

In *Anable v. Ford*, the high school involved had an extensive drug use policy stating that "A trace of illegal drugs/alcohol in one's body is a violation of this policy," and that students violating the policy could be required to submit to a variety of tests, including urinalysis (*Anable v. Ford*, 653 F. Supp. 22 (W.D. Ark. 1985)). One of the plaintiffs, Laura, had gone to the restroom with a friend, Faye, during class. When they arrived, another girl, Stephanie, was present. The girls' stories conflict, but all agreed that marijuana smoke was present in the restroom. When she left, Stephanie told a teacher she had smelled marijuana in the restroom. The teacher told the principal, and both proceeded to the restroom, where they confirmed the presence of marijuana smoke. The principal interviewed the three girls separately. Stephanie claimed that she had seen either Laura or Faye holding a joint, but all three girls denied smoking in the restroom. Although the defendants maintained they had told the girls that drug testing was optional, all three girls testified that they thought they were being forced to take urine tests. Because it was a Friday afternoon, the testing could not be scheduled until the following week. Each girl was taken to the restroom by a female staff member and made to urinate in a vial while squatting in the open, in the presence of the staff member. Laura sued, claiming that her Fourth Amendment rights had been violated (*Id.*).

The court found that the testing was unreasonable both at its inception and in its scope. The court began by noting that the urinalysis tested for whether the girls had *used* marijuana, not *possessed* it, yet the girls had not been accused of being under the influence of marijuana at school. The particular test used was "the least expensive test available for the detection of marijuana use," and its results were highly problematic. Most importantly, it could not establish the time of use, the amount of use, or the effect on the user. Thus, the test provided "no information as to whether any given student has used marijuana while at school, possessed marijuana at school, or was under the influence of marijuana at school" (*Id.* at 39). Sanctioning students based on the results of such a test "constitutes an improper attempt by school officials to regulate off-campus conduct unrelated to school order or discipline. ... To the extent that the test and policy attempts [*sic*] to regulate out of school conduct in no way affecting the school setting or the learning process," the scope of the search was unreasonable (*Id.* at 40).

The court then commented on the method in which the urine samples were collected. It found that requiring the girls to disrobe in front of a school official and to urinate into a small vial in an open place was an excessive intrusion on their legitimate expectations of privacy under the circumstances, and that such excessive intrusion was not justified by the needs being met. Before that level of invasiveness could ever be justified, the court said, there must be a "high probability" that the search would produce evidence of a violation of school rules or criminal law. Given that the urinalysis used was incapable of yielding evidence of illicit activity during school, that "high probability" did not exist, and the search was thus not justified at its inception (*Id.* at 41).

Whether educational institutions should implement generalized drug testing of the general student population, such as conducting randomized urinalysis tests, is a highly debated topic with little guidance from the courts. In allowing drug testing of student athletes in a high school where drug usage among athletes had become "rampant," the Supreme Court nonetheless "caution[ed] against the assumption that suspicionless drug testing will readily pass constitutional muster in other contexts" (*Vernonia Sch. Dist. 47J v. Acton*, 515 U.S. 646, 665 (1995)). As discussed below, holdings that allow drug testing of targeted groups of students are careful to differentiate the contexts in which testing will be allowed—such as in *Vernonia*—from the idea of mandatory testing of the student body at large. Other than as discussed below, schools attempting to implement suspicionless testing policies make themselves a target for complaints of unconstitutional policies.

SEARCHES OF GROUPS OF STUDENTS AND SCREENING SEARCHES

Generally

Increasingly, educational institutions use methods for searching the bodies of large numbers of students, such as metal detectors and drug-sniffing dogs. Such screening searches upon entry into the institution's grounds, although generalized searches, have been upheld in many courts (Rapp §9.08). Generalized searches are less likely to be found reasonable once students are within the bounds of the institution's property, unless evidence exists of some specific circumstances justifying the search. Thus, an institution cannot make random searches of students or their possessions simply due to basic safety concerns. (See, e.g., *Doe v. Little Rock Sch. Dist.*, 380 F.3d 349 (8th Cir. 2004).) In comparison, if the institution had received information that an unidentified student was seen carrying a weapon, a search of all students or their possessions is much more likely to be held reasonable, due to the special circumstances created by this information. (See, e.g., *Thompson v. Carthage Sch. Dist.*, 87 F.3d 979 (8th Cir. 1996).)

Surveillance and Recordings of Students

As previously discussed, no reasonable expectation of privacy can exist for items in "plain view." The same can generally be said for behavior occurring in a place where one has no reasonable expectation of privacy. The key is whether an expectation of privacy is reasonable, not whether the place itself is accessible to the public. (See, e.g., *Katz v. United States*, 389 U.S. 347, 351 (1967) [finding a reasonable expectation of privacy to exist in regard to phone conversations held in a public telephone booth, because what a person "seeks to preserve as private, even in an area accessible to the public, may be constitutionally protected"].) Combined with the role of an educational institution in ensuring the safety of its students, video (without audio) surveillance of students in most areas of a school will be allowed. This would include hallways, classrooms, busses, and school parking lots.

However, some areas will be considered private by their very nature, such as dressing rooms. Here, a student clearly has a reasonable expectation of privacy, and any planned surveillance would be subject to the *T.L.O.* reasonableness test.

Most court cases dealing with surveillance of students involve videotaping. At least one appellate court has succinctly stated, "Video surveillance is inherently intrusive" (*Brannum v. Overton County Sch. Bd.*, 516 F.3d 489, 496 (6th Cir. 2008)). In that case, video cameras had been installed in the locker rooms of a junior high school for the purpose of increasing safety. As the court emphasized, however, the school had no history of problems in the locker rooms, nor any indication that such problems would occur in the future. Although the installation of video cameras for the purpose of increasing security might have been reasonable at its inception, the scope of the intrusion was completely disproportionate to the needs being served. The court discussed at some length the balancing process required in applying the *T.L.O.* standard, noting that reasonableness can be measured by "the congruence or incongruence of the policy to be served (student safety), and the means adopted to serve it" (*Id.* at 497). Given the heightened level of privacy expectations in a school locker room, the court found that the use of video cameras was "incongruent to any demonstrated necessity, and wholly disproportionate to the claimed policy goal of assuring increased school security, especially when there is no history of any threat to security in the locker rooms" (*Id.* at 497–98).

Recording surveillances of students brings in additional considerations beyond the Fourth Amendment. Many states have laws specifically addressing the video and/or audio recording of minors by schools; such laws often apply to private as well as public schools. Note that state laws frequently treat surveillance and recordings with an audio component (whether audio only or audiovisual) differently than silent video. Based on a reasonable expectation of privacy in some conversations held even in publicly accessible places, state law is often much more restrictive on allowing surveillance and recordings that include audio. To the extent that recordings are considered "educational records," they may be subject to the Family Educational Rights and Privacy Act. However, the analysis of which types of surveillance recordings fall under FERPA is very fact-specific, and the question can be a murky one. For this reason, an institution's legal counsel should be consulted if the issue arises. The federal Electronic Communications Privacy Act could apply in some circumstances as well.

Beyond the legal implications, recording minors raises policy issues that are not raised by contemporaneous observation. As one commentator has stated, surveilling children, even when legal, is "ripe for problems," and videotaping the surveillance only increases that ripeness (Rapp 2012, §9.08). Before engaging in videotaping of any student surveillance, educational institutions should discuss the matter with their legal counsel and, where minors are involved, parents in the school community.

See also the discussion of recording surveillance in Chapter 7.

Drug Dogs

Various courts have held that an educational institution's use of drug dogs in searching student possessions is not unreasonable and thus constitutional. This assumes that the dog is highly trained and is handled by a professional, and that the student's belongings are not opened before the search. However, if the dog alerts on a container, such as a backpack, that will provide the reasonable suspicion necessary to then open and search the container (Rapp 2012 §9.08).

Using drug dogs to search students themselves, however, is a different issue, and the courts contradict each other in their holdings. The Seventh Circuit has held that using drug dogs to sniff the entire student body of a school was reasonable, given the drug problem at the school (*Doe v. Renfrow*, 631 F.2d 91 (7th Cir. 1980)). However, the Fifth Circuit held that sniffing students without individualized suspicion was an unreasonable invasion of privacy. Note that in that case, the court emphasized that the dogs' noses had touched each student and distinguished that situation from the one in *Renfrow* (*Horton v. Goose Creek Indep. Sch. Dist.*, 690 F.2d 470 (5th Cir. 1982)). It may be relevant that both of these cases were decided before the Supreme Court established the reasonableness standard for schools in *New Jersey v. T.L.O.* in 1985. In 1999, the Ninth Circuit relied on the *T.L.O.* standard to find the use of drug dogs to sniff students to be unconstitutional. The government interest being served did not justify the invasion of privacy, because there was no evidence of "a drug crisis or even a drug problem" at the institution (*B.C. v. Plumas Unified Sch. Dist.*, 192 F.3d 1260, 1268 (9th Cir. 1999)).

This, again, is an area in which some states have legislation. It is incumbent on the reader to know his or her local laws and to consult with the institution's legal counsel when necessary.

Drug Testing of Students Involved in Extracurricular Activities

The Supreme Court has upheld the constitutionality of mandatory urine drug tests for students participating in extracurricular activities, both athletic in nature and otherwise. In *Vernonia School District 47J v. Acton*, the school district's policy of drug testing student athletes was a response to an exponential increase in drug use amongst students during the 1980s and evidence that drug use was rampant among athletes, and was established only after the school had attempted to control the problem by other means, such as educating students about the dangers of drug use (515 U.S. 646 (1995)). In *Board of Education of Independent School District No. 92 of Pottawatomie County v. Lindsay Earls*, the district's policy required all students involved in competitive extracurricular activities to be drug tested, despite a lack of evidence of a significant drug problem in that district (536 U.S. 822 (2002)). Otherwise, the facts in both cases are very similar. In both, the students were required to consent to be tested before beginning participation in the programs, randomly throughout their participation, and upon reasonable suspicion. Specimen collection was conducted privately: Although a monitor was present, girls were allowed to urinate in a closed stall, and boys either in a closed stall or at a urinal while fully clothed. Independent companies tested the urine for the presence of illicit drugs (in *Earls*, also prescription drugs), and the results were tightly controlled, being shown only to those with a "need to know." Positive results were not reported to law enforcement, nor were students disciplined based on positive results, other than by having their ability to participate in extracurricular activities affected (515 U.S. 646 (1995); 536 U.S. 822 (2002)).

In both cases, the Court held that the students' reasonable expectation of privacy was limited. School children have a relatively low expectation of privacy to begin with, given the school's responsibility to protect their safety and health, including routine requirements of physical exams and vaccinations (*Vernonia*, 515 U.S. at 656; *Earls*, 536 U.S. at 830). In *Vernonia*, the Court pointed out that athletes have an even lower expectation of privacy, as they commonly undress and shower in each other's presence (515 U.S. at 657). In *Earls*, the Court pointed to varying requirements for different activities, which often include travel and "communal undress" (536 U.S. at 831).

In both cases, the Court held the character of intrusion to be minimal. The conditions of privacy in which specimens were collected was sufficient to protect the privacy of the student's body and bodily functions, and the degree of protection afforded to the results sufficiently safeguarded the privacy of information about the student's physical condition (*Vernonia*, 515 U.S. at 658; *Earls*, 536 U.S. at 832–34).

The Court next considered the nature and immediacy of the governmental concern at issue and the efficacy of the district's means of meeting that need. The Court in both cases referred to prior cases in which it had upheld drug testing of railroad employees and customs officials for the sake of protecting the public. The *Vernonia* Court expounded upon the detrimental effects of illicit drug use by maturing children, concluding that this problem "is an immediate crisis of greater proportions" than the dangers existing in the referenced cases (*Vernonia*, 515 U.S. at 663). Both Courts found the efficacy of the drug-testing programs to be self-evident. In both cases, the plaintiffs had argued that the district should employ a less intrusive policy of testing students only upon individualized suspicion of use. Both Courts pointed out that a policy limiting testing to individual students suspected of drug use might have the actual effect of being more intrusive than the programs currently employed, noting the danger that such testing could be used arbitrarily by teachers against troublesome but not drug-using students, the increased burdens of requiring teachers to identify potential drug users, and the increased expense of defending related lawsuits (*Vernonia*, 515 U.S. at 658; *Earls*, 536 U.S. at 837).

It is worth noting that the *Earls Court* emphasized that it had decided only the constitutionality, not the "wisdom" of drug testing in schools: "Within the limits of the Fourth Amendment, local school boards must assess the desirability of drug testing schoolchildren. ... [W]e express no opinion as to its wisdom" (536 U.S. at 838).

"SEIZURES": DETAINING STUDENTS FOR QUESTIONING AND OTHER REASONS

The Supreme Court has defined "seizure" under the Fourth Amendment as occurring when "a reasonable person would have believed that he was not free to leave" (*Michigan v. Chesternut*, 486 U.S. 567, 573 (1988)). In the educational context, most courts apply the same standard for seizures as for searches: the reasonableness standard articulated in *New Jersey v. T.L.O.* Thus, if the seizure was justified at its inception and reasonable in scope considering the circumstances, the constitutionality of the seizure will be upheld. The following examples will help to demonstrate how a court finds this balance.

The Third Circuit found the seizure of a high school student to be constitutional where that male student was accused of touching a female student in a sexual manner without her consent. The principal called the accused student into a small conference room, where he admitted to the sexual misconduct but claimed it was consensual. The principal then forced him to remain in the room for 3 hours and 45 minutes, while school officials investigated the incident and considered the appropriate punishment. During that time, the student was allowed to work on his homework and to leave the room to eat lunch and get a drink of water. The court found the detention to be reasonable under the circumstances, given the serious nature of the allegation (*Shuman v. Penn Manor Sch. Dist.*, 422 F.3d 141 (3d Cir. 2005)).

The Tenth Circuit applied the same standard to uphold a 20-minute detention of a student for questioning regarding a bomb threat made against the institution. The court held the questioning to be justified at its inception because other students had implicated the detained student in writing the letter and the scope of detention to be reasonably necessary to determine whether he had actually made the threat (*Edwards v. Rees*, 883 F.2d 882 (10th Cir. 1989)).

The Fifth Circuit upheld detaining a student who had been unruly on a field trip in a holding room of the juvenile detention facility being toured. The boy had repeatedly been told to behave himself when he acted up. When he continually refused, the teacher in charge asked for him to be placed in the holding room so that the others could continue the tour uninterrupted. The room contained only a bed and toilet and was continuously monitored. He was in the room for less than an hour. The court held the detention to be reasonable. It was justified at its inception because of the student's repeated refusal to behave and the need to separate him from the other students so that they could continue the tour. The scope of detention was reasonable given that due to the presence of the residents of the facility, some of whom were potentially dangerous, the student should not have been left alone; the room was relatively large, contained a bed and toilet, had a glass partition in the door, and was continuously monitored; the student was not otherwise restrained; and the detention lasted no longer than necessary, as he was released as soon as the tour concluded (*Hassan v. Lubbock Indep. Sch. Dist.*, 55 F.3d 1075 (5th Cir. 1995)).

In contrast, the California Supreme Court, noting that the freedom of students in school is already limited, has held that students may be detained so long as the official's conduct was not "arbitrary, capricious, or undertaken for purposes of harassment" (*In re Randy G.*, 28 P.3d 239, 245 (Cal. 2001)).

Another issue to arise in the context of seizures is the question of the amount of force that may lawfully be used to detain a student. The Supreme Court has held that the right to detain someone necessarily includes the right to use "reasonable force." (See, e.g., *Graham v. Connor*, 490 U.S. 386 (1989); *Muehler v. Mena*, 544 U.S. 93 (2005).) As always, the analysis of what constitutes "reasonable" is determined by the specific circumstances. For example, handcuffing a student to ensure the safety of others or to prevent the student from fleeing may be reasonable (*Hill v. Sharber*, 544 F. Supp. 2d 670 (M.D. Tenn. 2008)).

INVOLVING LAW ENFORCEMENT IN SCHOOL SEARCHES AND SEIZURES

Increasingly, law enforcement officers and institutional officials work together in the educational context. In their role as law enforcement, officers are held to a significantly higher standard of reasonableness in searches and seizures than are school officials. This is in part because of the purpose of such actions (the search for criminals), in part because of their specialized training, and in part because holding officials of educational institutions to such standards is impractical. A constitutional search by law enforcement usually requires a search warrant, which itself requires the existence of probable cause. However, since the less stringent *T.L.O.* standard of reasonableness applies to education officials, one must determine which standard should apply to law enforcement officials working in the educational setting.

Note that for purposes of this discussion, references to law enforcement officers refer to sworn public law enforcement individuals who are granted power by a governing body to keep the peace, such as the local police or sheriff departments; this discussion does not apply to any other category of individuals who may participate in providing security for an institution, such as private security services or volunteers. As a general statement, determining which standard of reasonableness will apply when educational officials work together with law enforcement is based on who is primarily in control of the search and/or seizure. That determination considers factors such as who initiates the search and for what purpose, who participates in the search/seizure, who makes decisions regarding whom to search and how, and whether the role served by the officer is more akin to that of law enforcement or school official.

This is true regardless of whether the law enforcement officer is employed as school security, assigned to the institution by the police department, or has any other defined relationship with the educational institution (Rapp 2012, §9.08).

For example, the lower standard of "reasonableness" set out in *T.L.O.* has been held applicable where students were called out of high school class by school officials at the request of police officers, who had learned of a planned after-school fight, and the students were detained and questioned in the vice principal's office by the officers and with the vice principal present. In this case, the court noted "The officers proceeded through school channels by using the Vice-Principal's power to summon the plaintiffs (and others) for interrogation and admonishment. Nothing was done that school officials could not have done themselves. Conversely, no more was done than necessary to discourage the fight" (*Milligan v. City of Slidell*, 226 F.3d 652, 655 (5th Cir. 2000)). Similarly, where students reported to a teacher that a classmate had brought a gun to school, the court upheld the school's detaining the 10-year-old in the principal's office for questioning by both school officials and law enforcement officers without first notifying a parent, stating, "School officials must have the leeway to maintain order on school premises and secure a safe environment in which learning can flourish. Over-constitutionalizing disciplinary procedures can undermine educators' ability to best attain these goals. [Holding for the plaintiff would] eviscerate the ability of administrators to meet the remedial exigencies of the moment" (*Wofford v. Evans*, 390 F.3d 318, 321 (4th Cir. 2004)).

Warrantless searches have also been allowed where officials of educational institutions have requested police involvement for the limited purpose of drawing upon the officers' expertise. For example, an arrest based on a warrantless search was upheld where university officials, upon receiving complaints of a strong "noxious" odor, searched a briefcase found in a student's locker, discovered what they suspected were packets of illegal drugs, consulted police only to confirm the accurate identification of the contents, and eventually turned the briefcase over to the police. The court noted, "What matters here is that until Deputy Saldivar was asked to examine the briefcase, its contents remained a mystery to the officials who bore the responsibility of properly disposing of it. The deputy's inspection therefore does not require justification over and above that of the continuing emergency which authorized the original warrantless search of defendant's locker" (*People v. Lantheir*, 5 Cal. 3d 751, 758 (1971)).

The key as to which standard to apply in a search involving both education officials and law enforcement officers is the degree of involvement of the officers, acting in their role as law enforcement. As one court put it, "When a law enforcement officer directs, participates, or acquiesces in a search conducted by private parties, that search must comport with [the higher standard of probable cause and obtaining a warrant]" (*M.J. v. State of Florida*, 399 So.

2d 996, 998 (Fla. Dist. Ct. App. 1981)). Comparing the following cases provides a good illustration of this principle.

In *M.J. v. State of Florida*, three students told the assistant principal, Mr. Black, that they had seen a bag of marijuana in M.J.'s underwear. Mr. Black called the police, and when Officer York arrived, called M.J. to his office. There, both men questioned M.J. for 10 minutes and demanded that he produce any marijuana in his possession. The men then told him that he would be arrested and that his uncle, also a police officer, would be called. At that point, M.J. said, "Don't call my uncle," and told the men they could search him. He then produced a marijuana cigarette from his coat pocket. M.J. denied Mr. Black's accusation of possessing more marijuana, at which point Officer York said he would call the uncle to meet them at the police station and that a search could be conducted. Mr. Black then told M.J. to pull down his pants, which he did; when Mr. Black said, "Go further," M.J. pulled a bag of marijuana out of his underwear. M.J. was arrested and subsequently convicted of delinquency (*Id.*).

The state argued that the lower standard of reasonableness should be used in assessing the constitutionality of the search. The court disagreed, stating that, "When a law enforcement officer directs, participates, or acquiesces in a search conducted by private parties, that search must comport with usual constitutional standards. Additionally, . . . the officer must have probable cause for that search, even though the school officials acting alone are treated as state officials subject to a lesser constitutional standard . . ." (*Id.*). The court went on to hold that, even if a warrant was not required, the simple reporting of three students to the assistant principal, without further corroboration, was insufficient to constitute probable cause (*Id.*).

In comparison, where the police officer involved played only a minor role, the U.S. District Court of Illinois found the search to be constitutional (*Martens v. District No. 220, Board of Educ.*, 620 F. Supp. 29 (N.D. Ill. 1985)). In that case, the high school dean of students received an anonymous call in which a woman identified herself as living in a certain neighborhood and said she had discovered marijuana cigarettes in her daughter's possession; that they had been purchased from James Lafollette, a student at the school; and that Lafollette kept marijuana in a Marlboro box in his locker. The dean had Lafollette open his locker, where she found a Marlboro box containing marijuana. Later in the day, the dean received another anonymous call, also from a woman identifying herself as living in the same neighborhood as the first caller, claiming that her daughter had bought marijuana cigarettes from James Lafollette and Michael Martens. She said that Martens kept drug paraphernalia in the lining of his coat. The dean called Martens to her office and confronted him. He denied possessing marijuana and refused to consent to a search without his parents present. The dean spent 45 minutes attempting to contact the parents, with no success. At that point, a sheriff's deputy, who was at the school on an unrelated matter, came into the dean's office. He told Martens that, based on his experience, it would be best to cooperate with school officials. He then asked Martens to empty his pockets, which he did, thus producing a pipe with marijuana residue. Martens was subsequently expelled for the rest of the year. However, the expulsion was not put on his permanent record or revealed to colleges or prospective employers, and no criminal charges were made (*Id.* at 30–31).

Martens's trial was held shortly after the *New Jersey v. T.L.O.* decision was issued. The court noted that the current case differed from *T.L.O.* by the presence of the law enforcement officer. However, the court found the officer's level of participation in the matter not to be significant enough to apply the higher standard of probable cause or requirement of a search warrant. "In short, [the officer's] urging was the immediate cause of Marten's emptying his pockets, but there is no indication that a criminal investigation was contemplated, that this was a cooperative effort with law enforcement, or that but for his intervention Martens would not have been searched eventually" (*Id.* at 32). The court went on to note that, given the officer's "limited role," the purpose served by application of the lower standard, described in *T.L.O.* as "preserving swift and informal disciplinary procedures," would not be served by imposing probable cause and warrant requirements in this case (*Id.*). It is interesting to note that the court went on to state that even though it was not required, probable cause probably had been established in this case, based on (1) the plausibility of the anonymous caller's tip being true, given a "substantial drug problem" at the school; (2) the presumptive credibility of the tip, since it came from a member of the public and not a police informant; and (3) the likelihood that the caller was the same as the earlier caller whose tip had been proved reliable (*Id.*).

EMERGENCIES MAY ALLOW DISCLOSING STUDENT INFORMATION

FERPA contains several exceptions to its protection of educational records that allow the release of records without consent. One of the most frequently used allows the release of records without consent "in connection with an emergency, appropriate persons if the knowledge of such information is necessary to protect the health or safety of the student or other persons," subject to regulations promulgated by the secretary of education (20 U.S.C. §1232g(b)(1)(I)). The decision of when it is appropriate to make such a disclosure and to whom should be made on a case-by-case basis by the educational institution (Family Educational Rights and Privacy Act, 34 C.F.R. 99.31 (2011)). The exception applies only when the situation presents imminent danger to the student to whom the information pertains, other students, or other members of the school community. The release must be narrowly tailored to meet the needs of the situation, including the immediacy, magnitude, and specificity of the information released, in the context of the danger presented (Dear Colleague Letter of LeRoy S. Rooker, Director, Family Policy Compliance Office, April 12, 2002, p. 3).

The most common situations likely to rise to this level include student illness, existence of a reason to believe a student will harm himself or others, and where the student is an apparent victim of abuse, although the Family Policy Compliance Office—the division of the Department of Education tasked with implementing FERPA—has made clear that events such as bioterrorist attacks would qualify (*Id.*).

It is important to keep in mind that the danger must be imminent. Thus, release of personal information without consent might be allowed in a situation dealing with the outbreak of an epidemic, such as H1N1 or *E. coli*, but would not be allowed to disclose the general health status of a student (Family Educational Rights and Privacy, 73 Fed. Reg. 237, 74,805 (Dec. 9, 2008) [to be codified at 34 C.F.R. pt. 99]). Since we now know that HIV/AIDS is not easily communicable in a classroom setting, it is highly unlikely that identification without consent of a student with HIV/AIDS would fall under the exception (Harty-Golder 1990, 55).

BIBLIOGRAPHY

Anable v. Ford, 653 F. Supp. 22 (W.D. Ark. 1985).

Anders v. Fort Wayne Cmty. Schs., 124 F. Supp. 2d 618 (N.D. Ind. 2000).

B.C. v. Plumas Unified Sch. Dist., 192 F.3d 1260 (9th Cir. 1999).

Board of Ed. of Indep. Sch. Dist. No. 92 of Pottawatomie County v. Lindsay Earls, 536 U.S. 822 (2002).

Brannum v. Overton County Sch. Bd., 516 F.3d 489 (6th Cir. 2008).

Doe v. Little Rock Sch. Dist., 380 F.3d 349 (8th Cir. 2004).

Doe v. Renfrow, 631 F.2d 91 (7th Cir. 1980).

Edwards v. Rees, 883 F.2d 882 (10th Cir. 1989).

Graham v. Connor, 490 U.S. 386 (1989).

Harty-Golder, J., *The Educator's Guide to AIDS: Law, Medicine, and Policy* (Asheville, NC: College Administration Publishers, Inc., 1990).

Hassan v. Lubbock Indep. Sch. Dist., 55 F.3d 1075 (5th Cir. 1995).

Hedges v. Musco, 204 F.3d 109 (3d Cir. 2000).

Hill v. Sharber, 544 F. Supp. 2d 670 (M.D. Tenn. 2008).

Horton v. Goose Creek Indep. Sch. Dist., 690 F.2d 470 (5th Cir. 1982).

In re Randy G., 28 P.3d 239, 245 (Cal. 2001).

Jenkins ex rel. Hall v. Talladega City Bd. of Educ., 95 F.3d 1046 (11th Cir. 1996).

Katz v. United States, 389 U.S. 347 (1967).

Martens v. District No. 220, Board of Educ., 620 F. Supp. 29 (N.D. Ill. 1985).

Michigan v. Chesternut, 486 U.S. 567 (1988).

Milligan v. City of Slidell, 226 F.3d 652 (5th Cir. 2000).

M.J. v. State of Florida, 399 So. 2d 996 (Fla. Dist. Ct. App. 1981).

Muehler v. Mena, 544 U.S. 93 (2005).

New Jersey v. T.L.O., 469 U.S. 325, 341 (1985).

People v. Lantheir, 5 Cal. 3d 751, 758 (1971).

People v. Overton, 229 N.E.2d 596 (N.Y. 1967).

Rapp, James, *Education Law* (New York: Matthew Bender & Co., 2012).

Safford Unified Sch. Dist. v. Redding, 557 U.S. 364 (2009).

Shuman v. Penn Manor Sch. Dist., 422 F.3d 141 (3rd Cir. 2005).

State v. Joseph T., 336 S.E.2d 728 (W. Va. 1985).

State v. Williams, 791 N.E.2d 608 (Ill. App. 2003).

Thompson v. Carthage Sch. Dist., 87 F.3d 979 (8th Cir. 1996).

Vernonia School District 47J v. Acton, 515 U.S. 646 (1995).

Wofford v. Evans, 390 F.3d 318, 321 (4th Cir. 2004).

Zamora v. Pomeroy, 639 F.2d 662 (10th Cir. 1981).

CHAPTER 6

Student Privacy Online

A comprehensive study conducted by the Pew Internet & American Life Project in 2007 found that 93 percent of Americans between the ages of 12 and 17 had used the Internet, with 61 percent using it daily (Lenhart and Madden 2007, 3). A 2010 Pew study found that 75 percent of children between the ages of 12 and 17 own a cell phone, and those teens would rather use the phone to text their friends than to call and talk to them. Of teenagers who own a cell phone, 88 percent—or, as the study points out, 72 percent of all teenagers—use text messaging, more than half of them on a daily basis (Lenhart et al. 2010, 2). The same study found that even though most schools attempt to regulate phone usage, 43 percent of teens who take their phones to school text in class at least once each day. Although 24 percent of teenagers attend schools that ban cell phones from school grounds entirely, 65 percent of these teens bring their phones to school every day anyway (*Id.* at 4). Even younger children are more likely to be involved in electronic communications than not. A 2012 study found that 56 percent of children in the United States between the ages of 8 and 12 own their own cell phones, 96 percent of which include texting and/or Internet capabilities (National Consumers League 2012). Of all Facebook users aged 18 and under, 38 percent are under the age of 13 (in violation of Facebook's policies) (MinorMonitor 2012).

On the privacy front, federal legislation is hopelessly out of sync with modern technology. States are just now beginning to legislate rights associated with data and information transmitted by and stored on cell phones, social media, and other electronic means. In 2012, Delaware became the first state to provide legislative protection for postsecondary students in both public and private schools, prohibiting schools from requiring access to a student's social media accounts (Del. Code Ann. tit.14 § 81 (2012)).

Absent specific legislation, educational institutions must rely on the same types of analyses discussed previously in non-technological settings, primarily the Fourth Amendment prohibition against unreasonable search and seizure and state tort law restricting invasion of privacy. As in any other area, the analysis boils down to whether the individual has a reasonable expectation of privacy in the items searched or seized and, if so, whether the public institution's interest in invading that privacy outweighs the invasion.

THE INTERSECTION OF FIRST AND FOURTH

Many cases addressing online privacy will necessarily implicate the First Amendment protection of free speech, because online activity often constitutes some level of expression. The unreasonable search or seizure of private expressions, regardless of the medium in which they are expressed, creates a chilling effect on the right to freely express ourselves. For this reason, courts may consider the potential for a chilling effect as part of the harm caused by an invasion of privacy in their determination of what constitutes a reasonable search or seizure: "We examine what is 'unreasonable' in the light of the values of freedom of expression" (*Roaden v. Kentucky*, 413 U.S. 496, 504 (1973)).

EMAIL, SOCIAL MEDIA, AND CELL PHONES: STUDENTS HAVE A REASONABLE EXPECTATION OF PRIVACY

Several courts have made clear that an individual has a reasonable expectation of privacy in his or her private email accounts and that the Fourth Amendment thus protects those rights. Although the Supreme Court has not yet confronted the question of email privacy, it has a long history of providing Fourth Amendment protection to the content of letters and packages sent through the mail. (See, e.g., *United States v. Jacobsen*, 466 U.S. 109 (1984).)

The landmark case of *Katz v. United States* firmly established that Fourth Amendment protections against unreasonable search and seizure are not limited to cases of intrusion on a physical place. In that 1967 case, the FBI had wiretapped a public phone booth without first obtaining a warrant. At trial, the FBI argued that the Fourth Amendment was not applicable because no physical intrusion had occurred. The Supreme Court disagreed, famously stating, "the Fourth Amendment protects people, not places. What a person knowingly exposes to the public, even in his own home or office, is not a subject of Fourth Amendment protection. But what he seeks to preserve as private, even in an area accessible to the public, may be constitutionally protected" (*Katz v. United States*, 389 U.S. 347, 351 (1967)). The Court noted that an expectation of privacy in a phone call made from a booth that can be shut off so that one cannot be heard outside of the booth is reasonable and held that the Fourth Amendment had been violated (*Id.* at 359).

Building on these lines of cases, multiple courts have confirmed a reasonable expectation of privacy in one's private emails. "Given the fundamental similarities between email and traditional forms of communication, it would defy common sense to afford emails lesser *Fourth Amendment* protection" (*United States v. Warshak*, 631 F.3d 266, 285–86 (6th Cir. 2010)). "The privacy interests in these two forms of communication [email and traditional mail] are identical" (*United States v. Forrester*, 512 F.3d 500, 511 (9th Cir. 2008)). The Fifth Circuit specifically found a reasonable expectation of privacy in "private information, including emails" stored on a cell phone (*United States v. Zavala*,

541 F.3d 562, 577 (5th Cir. 2008)). As discussed below, we are now beginning to see litigation regarding the privacy of social media accounts and information posted on social media tools.

The "Special Nature" of Cell Phones and Other Personal Electronic Devices

Although not banning students from carrying cell phones, the Nazareth Area School District prohibited "use or display" of cell phones during school hours. When a student's phone fell out of his pocket during class, the teacher confiscated the phone. The teacher, together with the assistant principal, then used the phone to call the student's friends, in an effort to determine whether they would violate the policy by answering the calls. They accessed the student's text messages and voice mail, discovering a message they believed referred to drug usage; and, finally, used his instant messenger to carry on a conversation with the student's younger brother, without identifying themselves (*Klump v. Nazareth Area Sch. Dist.*, 425 F. Supp. 2d 622 (E.D. Penn. 2006)).

Although the school was justified in seizing the phone, since displaying the phone had violated school policy, the court quickly found that the defendants had infringed the student's Fourth Amendment rights by searching his private messages. The court held that the search had not been justified at its inception, as the school had no reasonable ground for believing that the search would produce evidence the student had violated either the law or school policy (*Id.* at 640).

The *Klump* case spotlights the unique nature of cell phones and other electronic devices—which today all function as personal computers to some extent—in the context of students' privacy rights in their personal belongings by differentiating between the physical phone and the information contained on the phone. The Supreme Court's standard of what constitutes a reasonable search of student belongings as established in *New Jersey v. T.L.O.* was decided in 1985. That case addressed searching a student's purse. Other cases have upheld searches of student pockets, backpacks, and other similar items, as well as school property in which students may keep personal belongings, such as lockers and desks, so long as the *T.L.O.* reasonableness standard is met (Rapp 2012, §9.08). However, these items all differ in one significant way from cell phones: Cell phones are capable of containing amounts of data and information exponentially beyond the limits of these other items. Should a different standard apply to searches of the contents of phones?

A growing number of scholars, advocates, and even courts think so. As one commentator explains, an assumption underlying the Court's decision in *T.L.O.* is that students are necessarily limited in the amount of personal property they can carry to school, restricted by the size of a purse or backpack; or store on school grounds, restricted by the size of a locker (Spung 2011, 137). Cell phones, in comparison—as well as tablets, laptops, and other computing devices that students have legitimate reason to bring to school—contain a seemingly limitless amount of storage capacity. Furthermore, the type of information stored on these devices is very likely to include personal information, including personal information about other people, such as the student's family members. Even if possible, it is not practical to partition off certain sets of information on these devices, nor is it often practical for a student to own multiple phones or other devices, with one dedicated to school and one to personal use (*Id.* at 138).

Although many courts disagree, a few courts have recognized the concerns raised by the unique nature of cell phones. A California district court has held that a warrantless search of the contents of a cell phone by police officers violated the defendant's Fourth Amendment rights. In that case, police had the right to search the defendant and any "closed containers" concealed on her, because warrants are not required for these searches that are "incident to arrest." However, the defendant argued that her cell phone was not analogous to the type of closed container envisioned by the applicable law, because of its ability to contain a large amount of personal information. The court distinguished earlier cases that had considered electronic devices to be analogous to closed containers, in part based on the great advances in cell phone technology since those cases were decided in the 1990s. The court held that police must first obtain a warrant before searching the contents of a cell phone, stating that "their ability to store large amounts of private data gives their users a reasonable and justifiable expectation of a higher level of privacy in the information they contain" (*State of Ohio v. Smith*, 920 N.E.2d 949, 955 (Ohio 2009)). Note, however, that this holding is not typical, and the treatment of searches of cell phones varies amongst the courts.

Other cases have considered the question of whether laptops should be given a higher standard of privacy protection. In the criminal context, the courts are split as to whether a warrant must be obtained before searching the contents of a computer (Carucci et al. 2011). Although the issue was not before it, the Tenth Circuit wondered whether "one might speculate whether the Supreme Court would treat laptop computers, hard drives, flash drives or even cell phones as it has a briefcase or give those types of devices preferred status because of their unique ability to hold vast amounts of diverse personal information" (*United States v. Burgess*, 576 F.3d 1078 (10th Cir. 2009)).

In another context, the Fourth Circuit has analogized password-protected laptops to locked footlockers. One exception to the Fourth Amendment says law enforcement does not need a warrant when a person who shares a space with the subject of a search, such as his or her roommate, gives consent for the space to be searched. The concept supporting this exception is that since the roommate may allow anyone into the space without obtaining the subject's consent, anything the subject leaves lying out is considered to be in "plain view" for anyone who lawfully enters the space. However, that consent is limited by the "plain view" doctrine and does not cover searching inside closed containers, especially if they are locked, indicating that, unlike those items the subject leaves lying in plain view, he or she has an expectation of privacy for the items inside the container. In this context, the Fourth Circuit said that password-protected files are like locked footlockers, in that they indicate the subject's intention to keep the contents private from the roommate (*Id.*). Other courts have cited this reasoning in their own holdings under similar circumstances. (See, e.g., *United States v. Andrus*, 483 F.3d 711 (10th Cir. 2007).)

Some courts have suggested that while a police officer was justified in turning on a computer and observing the opening screen without first obtaining a warrant, a warrant might be needed before searching the contents of the computer. (See, e.g., *State of Kansas v. Stone*, No. 94770, 2007 Kan. App. Unpub. LEXIS 529 (Kan. Ct. App. 2007).)

To date, no cases have dealt squarely with the question of whether a heightened standard should be applied in the context of searching the contents of student phones or other devices. In both *T.L.O.* and *Safford v. Redding*, discussed in Chapter 5, the Supreme Court emphasized that the scope of a student search is reasonable only "when the measures adopted are reasonably related to the objectives of the search and not excessively intrusive in light of . . . the nature of the infraction" (*New Jersey v. T.L.O.*, 469 U.S. 325, 342 (1985)). Given the conflicting positions of the courts, the lack of case law regarding students, and the increasing push to limit an institution's ability to search the contents of student devices, educational institutions should consult with their legal counsel before making decisions and policies regarding the contents of students' electronic devices, if doing so at all.

Note that as of December 2012, Congress is considering a bill that would require law enforcement officers to obtain a warrant before accessing electronic messages stored on personal electronic devices. Should a version of that bill pass into law, it will certainly affect court analyses of student rights in the same devices.

OFF-CAMPUS ACTIVITIES

For an educational institution to be allowed to regulate the off-campus actions—including speech—of its students, the institution must be able to show that the activity it wishes to regulate would "materially and substantially disrupt the work and discipline of the school" (*Morse v. Frederick*, 551 U.S. 393, 404 (2007)). Thus, the Eighth Circuit upheld a school's suspension of a student when he texted a friend, outside of the school grounds and school hours, suggesting that he wanted to shoot particular students in the school. The court's decision was based on several factors, including the boy's admitted depression, his claim to have access to weapons, and the actual disruption caused when his texts became known and students and parents began to call the principal asking about a rumored "hit list" (*D.J.M. v. Hannibal Pub. Sch. Dist.* #60, 647 F.3d 754 (8th Cir. 2011)).

If it is not reasonable to believe that the student's speech would cause such a drastic disruption of school activities, a school that punishes a student for his or her protected speech made off-campus, no matter how offensive to the school or its employees, infringes that student's First Amendment rights. Courts have found a student's First Amendment rights to have been infringed when the high school disciplined the student for creating a profile of the school principal on MySpace featuring "malicious and inflammatory statements," profanity, and "shameful personal attacks on the principal and his family." Despite the "unfortunate humiliation" to the principal, the profiles simply did not cause substantial disruption of or material interference with school activities (*Layshock v. Hermitage Sch. Dist.*, 650 F.3d 205 (3d Cir. 2011); *J.S. ex rel. Snyder v. Blue Mountain Sch. Dist.*, 650 F.3d 915 (3d Cir. 2011)). In comparison, a school may be able to prevent a high school student from running for election to student office—a voluntary, extracurricular activity—based on her out-of-school blog posting criticizing school officials and referring to them as "douchebags" if it is foreseeable that other students and administrators would become aware of the posting (*Doninger v. Niehoff*, 642 F.3d 334 (2d Cir. 2011)).

In a recently decided case, a district court confirmed that Facebook users have a reasonable expectation of privacy in the materials they post and held that a high school violated a student's First and Fourth Amendment rights when it required her to provide login information for her account and then disciplined her based on the content of private messages she had sent and postings to her Facebook wall (*R.S. v. Minnewaska Area Sch. Dist.*, 2012 U.S. Dist. LEXIS 126257 (Dist. Minn. 2012)). In that case, the sixth-grade student had posted on her Facebook wall saying she hated Kathy, an adult hall monitor at her school, because Kathy had been mean to her. A friend who saw the message copied it and showed it to the principal, who sent R.S. to detention. She later posted on her wall, "I want to know who the f%$# [*sic*] told on me." That also came to the principal's attention, and she was punished again. A few weeks later, the guardian of a male student complained to school officials that the boy had received messages on sexual topics "via the Internet" from R.S. The school counselor talked to R.S., who admitted to sending the messages off of school grounds and outside of school hours. She was then called to meet with a deputy sheriff who was assigned to the school and other school officials, who demanded that she give them the user names and passwords for her email and Facebook accounts. When she claimed to not remember them, she was threatened with detention. She gave them the information, and the officials spent 15 minutes searching her Facebook account and email, including private messages sent through Facebook. The counselor called R.S.'s mother, but R.S. was not punished by the school (*Id.*).

The court first addressed R.S.'s First Amendment rights, noting, "The movement of student speech to the internet poses some new challenges, but that transition has not abrogated the clearly established general principles which have governed schools for decades." (*Id.* at *19–20) Finding that R.S.'s messages were not likely to cause a substantial disruption in school activities, the court held that the school had infringed her First Amendment rights (*Id.* at *23).

The court then turned to R.S.'s claim of infringement of her Fourth Amendment rights. It held that R.S. had a reasonable expectation of privacy in her private Facebook information and messages, citing cases that had found a right of privacy in private emails and private Facebook messages (*Id.* at *30–31). The court held that the school had infringed R.S.'s privacy rights under the Fourth Amendment, because it lacked a legitimate reason to engage in the searches of her accounts, noting that the search did not appear to be motivated by a concern with maintaining discipline in the classroom, nor did the officials have any reason to expect the search would uncover evidence of illegal activities or violations of school policy (*Id.* at *33).

INTEGRATING SOCIAL MEDIA AND OTHER INTERACTIVE TECHNOLOGY INTO THE CURRICULUM

Social media and other interactive technologies (which, for simplicity's sake, I will refer to collectively as "Web 2.0 technology") can serve as valuable instructional tools. Educational institutions at all levels have recognized this and are beginning to integrate Web 2.0 technology into their curriculum and classroom activities. As is true with all tools, however, one must use it knowledgeably and carefully for it to be not only effective, but safe. A variety of concerns arise in connection with using Web 2.0 technology in the educational context, with the primary areas of concern being cyberbullying, cyberstalking, predation of children, copyright infringement by students and educators, and privacy vulnerabilities. However, if these concerns can be adequately addressed, using Web 2.0 technology as part of the instructional process can open entire new realms of possibilities.

Since the primary object of protection is the student, students themselves need to be trained in how to protect themselves and their privacy in this environment. Not only minors, but postsecondary students as well, often lack the maturity necessary to understand the ramifications of their actions. For example, in the Facebook context, a user chooses which individuals may view his or her postings, and all others are restricted from the user's page. However, the original posting is easily reposted by an approved "friend," and their friends, and their friends. We have no way to truly control what happens to anything posted on any social media. Furthermore, even when a user has removed a posting, it may continue to exist in caches and archives of search engines (Barr and Lugus 2011). The results of polls repeatedly show that a significant proportion of employers search the Internet to find information about applicants, and that what they find on social networking sites can influence their hiring decisions. (See, e.g., MedZilla 2007.) Young people are certainly not the only ones to disregard this reality, but they are particularly vulnerable to not understanding the potential effects.

Before leaping into the Web 2.0 technology, the educational institution should think through how it will use these tools, prepare a policy, and train educators and administrators. Consider questions such as what are the goals to be served, what risks are involved, and how will the institution mitigate the risks? The answers to these questions will be different for every institution and, in particular, will vary in regard to the age and level of students. Where minors are involved, the institution should consider including parents in these conversations.

Collecting Student Data and Works

Every educational institution should work with its legal counsel to establish and abide by a policy defining what types of information it will collect from students online, how it will protect the information in the process of collection as well as in storage, and how it will and will not use that information. Keep in mind FERPA requirements and limitations. Consider not only personal data such as personally identifying information, but any materials that may reveal personal information about students. For example, applications for admissions usually require some type of personal statement. Increasingly, students submit assignments online. Students may create digital works, such as videos, mash-ups, and other multimedia works, that they'll want to share online; in many cases, however, these works will include information about other students. Even the traditional student newspaper, overseen by faculty, if made openly available online suddenly raises significant privacy issues. All of these types of situations should be considered and discussed, and policies written to clarify how the institution intends to address these situations.

BIBLIOGRAPHY

Barr, Jamison, and Emmy Lugus, "Digital Threats on Campus: Examining the Duty of Colleges to Protect Their Social Networking Students," 33 *W. New Eng. L. Rev.* 757 (2011).

Carucci, Dominic, David Overhuls, and Nicholas Soares, "Computer Crimes," 48 Am. Crim. L. Rev. 375 (2011).

Consumer Reports, "That Facebook Friend Might Be 10 Years Old, and Other Troubling News," http://www.consumerreports.org/cro/magazine-archive/2011/june/electronics-computers/state-of-the-net/facebook-concerns/index.htm (June 2012).

D.J.M. v. Hannibal Pub. Sch. Dist. #60, 647 F.3d 754 (8th Cir. 2011).

Doninger v. Niehoff, 642 F.3d 334 (2d Cir. 2011).

J.S. ex rel. Snyder v. Blue Mountain Sch. Dist., 650 F.3d 915 (3d Cir. 2011).

Katz v. United States, 389 U.S. 347, 351 (1967).

Klump v. Nazareth Area Sch. Dist., 425 F. Supp. 2d 622 (E.D. Penn. 2006).

Layshock v. Hermitage Sch. Dist., 650 F.3d 205 (3d Cir. 2011).

Lenhart, Amanda, Rich Ling, Scott Campbell, and Kristen Purcell, "Teens and Mobile Phones," http://www.pewinternet.org/~/media/Files/Reports/2010/PIP -Teens-and-Mobile-2010-with-topline.pdf (April 20, 2010).

Lenhart, Amanda, and Mary Madden, "Teens, Privacy, and Online Social Networks," http://www.pewinternet.org/~/media/Files/Reports/2007/PIP_Teens_Privacy_SNS _Report_Final.pdf.pdf (April 18, 2007).

MedZilla, "The Growing Problem of Digital Dirt," http://www.medzilla.com/ press200705-528402.html (May 23, 2007).

MinorMonitor, "Kids Safety on Facebook," http://www.minormonitor.com/ infographic/kids-on-facebook/ (April 20, 2012).

Morse v. Frederick, 551 U.S. 393 (2007).

National Consumers League, "Survey: Majority of 'Tweeners' Now Have Cell Phones, with Many Parents Concerned about Cost," http://www.nclnet.org/ newsroom/press-releases/681-survey-majority-of-tweeners-now-have-cell-phones -with-many-parents-concerned-about-cost (July 10, 2012).

New Jersey v. T.L.O., 469 U.S. 325 (1985).

Rapp, James, *Education Law* (New York: Matthew Bender & Co., 2012).

Roaden v. Kentucky, 413 U.S. 496 (1973).

R.S. v. Minnewaska Area Sch. Dist., 2012 U.S. Dist. LEXIS 126257 (Dist. Minn. 2012).

Spung, A. James, "From Backpacks to BlackBerries: (Re)Examining *New Jersey v. T.L.O.* in the Age of the Cell Phone," 61 *Emory L. J.* 111 (2011).

State of Kansas v. Stone, No. 94770, 2007 Kan. App. Unpub. LEXIS 529 (Kan. Ct. App. 2007).

State of Ohio v. Smith, 920 N.E.2d 949 (Ohio 2009).

Trulock v. Freeh, 275 F.3d 391 (4th Cir. 2001).

United States v. Andrus, 483 F.3d 711 (10th Cir. 2007).

United States v. Burgess, 576 F.3d 1078 (10th Cir. 2009).

United States v. Forrester, 512 F.3d 500 (9th Cir. 2008).

United States v. Jacobsen, 466 U.S. 109 (1984).

United States v. Warshak, 631 F.3d 266 (6th Cir. 2010).

United States v. Zavala, 541 F.3d 562 (5th Cir. 2008).

CHAPTER 7

Faculty and Staff Rights to Privacy

Faculty and staff at all levels are accorded rights under the Constitution as well as under statutory law. Rights of employees and employers arising from statutory law are primarily at the state law level, which varies greatly from state to state. Relevant laws may address specific technology or situations, or may fall under the greater area of labor and employment law. Some may apply only to public employees, others to all employees or all citizens of the state. Further, the employee-employer relationship may be governed by contract and/or union status. Thus, it is incumbent on the reader to know and understand the significance of the factors relevant to his or her situation.

THE FOURTH AMENDMENT AND AN EMPLOYER'S RIGHT TO SEARCH EMPLOYEES' THINGS

Public employees are protected by the Fourth Amendment from unreasonable searches and seizures, even in their role as employees. State tort law regulates protection granted to private employees and may provide greater or more specific protection to public employees than found under the Fourth Amendment. However, the role of employee may limit the protection somewhat in that it defines the reasonableness of searches and seizures.

Even the Supreme Court has noted its surprise at the dearth of case law on Fourth Amendment protection against searches of a public employee's workspace when it considered the issue in a 1987 decision regarding a public hospital administrator whose office had been searched by hospital staff while he was placed on administrative leave. The administrator had stolen a computer from the hospital and was accused of other misconduct, including sexual harassment of some employees. He was put on administrative leave, during which time his office, desk, and file cabinet were searched multiple times by staff, apparently in attempts to find items related to the allegations against him. The Court applied the reasonableness standard articulated in *New Jersey v. T.L.O.*, requiring that the search be reasonable in its inception and scope (*O'Connor v. Ortega*, 480 U.S. 709 (1987)). (See Chapter 5 for further discussion of this standard.)

The issues before the Court were (1) whether a public employee has a reasonable expectation of privacy in his or her office, desk, and file cabinets; and (2) the appropriate standard to apply in determining whether the search violated the employee's Fourth Amendment rights. The Court first defined a "workplace" as "those areas and items that are related to work and are generally within the employer's control," noting that "[t]hese areas remain part of the workplace context even if the employee has placed personal items in them" (*Id.* at 722). The Court then held that, based on the circumstances, the administrator did indeed have an expectation of privacy in his workplace, citing, among other factors, that he did not share his desk or file cabinets with other employees, and he had occupied the office for 17 years and kept various personal items there during that time. In comparison, the Court noted that in other employment situations, individuals may regularly come and go to and from an employee's office, share workspace or storage space, and even go through each other's files when certain materials are needed; in this type of situation, it is unlikely that an employee would have a reasonable expectation of privacy (*Id.* at 718–19).

The Court then worked to define what would constitute an appropriate standard of reasonableness for a search in this context, confirming that this decision requires "balancing the nature and quality of the intrusion . . . against the importance of the governmental interests alleged to justify the intrusion" (*Id.* at 720). In its analysis, again noting that employers or other employees often need to enter a certain office, desk, or file cabinet for legitimate, work-related purposes, the Court emphasized that when the employer is a public employer, as is the case in many educational settings, the governmental interest includes the need for efficiently operating the workplace so as to best serve the public. Thus, it concluded, public employers must be given wide latitude to enter employee offices for work-related reasons, including those related to an investigation of alleged misbehavior by an employee. The implementation of the search, however, must be reasonable in its inception and its scope. A search is reasonable in its inception if conducted for purely work-related reasons, such as retrieving a file, or in the case of investigating employee misconduct, when reasonable grounds exist for suspecting that the search will reveal evidence related to the investigation. The scope will be reasonable where the search as carried out is reasonably related to the objectives of the search and not unnecessarily intrusive (*Id.* at 726).

Note that the analysis of the *O'Connor* Court is very similar to the analysis of whether students have a reasonable expectation of privacy in the private possessions they store in school property such as lockers. Similarly, subsequent cases have found no reasonable expectation of privacy where the employee did not have sole access to the workspace at issue. (See, e.g., *Shaul v. Cherry Valley-Springfield Cent. Sch. Dist.*, 363 F.3d 177 (2d Cir. 2004); *United States v. Buettner-Janusch*, 646 F.2d 759 (2d Cir. 1981); *People v. Powell*, 599 N.W.2d 499 (Mich. Ct. App. 1999).) Others have found a reasonable expectation of privacy to exist where the workspace was indeed controlled by the employee, such as for a locked desk when no notice was given of the search (*Schowengerdt v. General Dynamics Corp.*, 823 F.2d 1328 (9th Cir. 1987)) or the desk of a school guidance counselor absent a practice of or policy for allowing searches, such as might be stated in an employee manual or handbook (*Gillard v. Schmidt*, 579 F.2d 825 (3d Cir. 1978)). However, since the circumstances determine whether a reasonable expectation of privacy exists, if the circumstances change, the reasonableness of an expectation of privacy may change as well. One court has held that although a teacher might have originally had a reasonable expectation of privacy in his personal belongings kept in his classroom and a locked cabinet, he lost that expectation when he returned the key to the cabinet and was given the opportunity to remove his personal belongings (*Shaul*, 363 F.3d 177).

SURVEILLANCE OF THE WORKPLACE

Recall that a reasonable expectation of privacy does not exist for items "in plain view." This is usually true for behavior that occurs in places open to the public view as well, in some cases even when the observer must go to great lengths to obtain his view, such as in the Supreme Court case involving police officers using a helicopter to circle above a greenhouse with an opening in the roof for the purpose of determining whether marijuana was being grown there. (See *Florida v. Riley*, 488 U.S. 445 (1989).) At least one court has specifically held that a public school classroom is a public place and, as such, no reasonable expectation of privacy exists. Note, however, that the court distinguished between the ability of the educational institution to make audio recordings of what happened in the classroom and an expectation of privacy in a teacher's desk and locked file cabinets within the classroom. Although the latter were not at issue in the case, the court noted that society might recognize a reasonable expectation of privacy in such articles (*Plock v. Board of Ed.*, 545 F. Supp. 2d 755 (N.D. Ill. 2007)).

Thus, covert surveillance of public areas, including break rooms, generally will not constitute a violation of Fourth Amendment protection. Nonetheless, if the institution plans to surveil employees in such places, it is good policy to inform employees so that all parties have the same understanding of rights and expectations.

Telephone Conversations

Although exceptions may exist under state laws, employers usually are prohibited from listening in on employee telephone calls. The major exception is when consent is deemed to have been given. Note that state law varies greatly, and many states require consent only by one party to the conversation; under those laws, consent is deemed to exist even if the other party is not aware that the call is being monitored or recorded. Further, consent may be implied, in which case the scope of the consent is determined based on the details of the situation. For example, where employees are put on notice that phone calls made on employer phones may be monitored, or even recorded, the employee will be deemed to have consented, but even that will be limited to what is included in the notice. If an employee handbook states that business calls may be monitored, consent has not been given for the monitoring of personal calls. (See *Watkins v. L. M. Berry & Co.*, 704 F.2d 577 (11th Cir. 1983).)

Recordings of Surveillance: Audio, No; Silent Video, Maybe

Recall from Chapter 2 that the Electronic Communications Privacy Act accords different types of restrictions to interception and recording of communications, based on the type of communication and the medium used to transmit the communication. Title I of the ECPA, also known as the Wiretap Act, generally prohibits secretly recording oral communications, including video that includes sound (18 U.S.C. §§2510–22). Some state statutes also prohibit such recordings. However, video recordings without sound do not violate the ECPA.

Several courts have upheld recorded surveillance within the educational context where sound was not recorded, usually to monitor illegal activity. Note that these cases involved monitoring of areas where no expectation of privacy applied, because the areas were accessible to multiple individuals, such as the use of a hidden video camera to record a university police officer gambling in an office used by all the university police officers to conduct public business (Rapp 2012, §6.09).

Consistent with the previously discussed cases in which no expectation of privacy was found in a place to which the plaintiff did not control access, the Supreme Judicial Court of Massachusetts found no expectation of privacy in such a place even when the plaintiff was there alone. In that case, a state college had installed hidden video cameras—with no sound recording capabilities—to monitor a work area that had been subject to after-hours theft. Multiple individuals had keys to the area. The plaintiff had used the area to change clothes before and after work hours; and, during a period in which she suffered severe sunburn, to partially disrobe to apply ointment to her burns. When she learned of the videotaping, she sued. The court held that she had no reasonable expectation of privacy because so many others had access to the area, despite the fact that no one else was present when she undressed (*Nelson v. Salem State Coll.*, 845 N.E.2d 338 (Mass. 2006)).

PHYSICAL AND PSYCHOLOGICAL TESTING

An educational institution may require employees to undergo physical or psychological examinations so long as the purpose of the test is related to their ability to perform their job, job performance, or conduct in the workplace. The examinations should be limited to only what is necessary to determine the employee's ability to perform his or her job and should be no more invasive than necessary. Many states have laws regulating this issue, which differ in the requirements an educational institution must fulfill (Rapp 2012, §6.11). As always, having a clear policy on the issue can help prevent problems.

Drug Testing

Little statutory law allows for the discipline or dismissal of educators based solely upon use or possession of illegal or controlled substances. Rather, additional factors must also exist. If the person's work performance is affected by the drug use, or by notoriety attached to public knowledge of the use, he or she may be disciplined for that reason. A caretaker of young children who is under the effects of drugs while the children are in his or her custody may be disciplined as a matter of public policy. If an employee violates the terms of his or her employment by using drugs, he or she may be disciplined on that basis. Thus, the most effective means of addressing concerns with employee drug use may be to address the issue in employee contracts or policies (Rapp 2012, §6.14).

In most cases, reasonable suspicion of possible drug use by the employee to be tested must exist. Reasonable suspicion is determined based on the circumstances and requires an objective evaluation of the facts, and it must be based on more than the occurrence of daily accidents, such as injuring oneself on the job. (See, e.g., *Reno v. East Baton Rouge Parish Sch. Bd.*, 697 F. Supp. 2d 659 (M.D. La. 2010).) Similarly, the Fifth Circuit found unconstitutional a board policy requiring employees injured on the job to be drug tested (*United Teachers of New Orleans v. Orleans Parish Sch.* Bd., 142 F.3d 853 (5th Cir. 1998)). Courts have also found unconstitutional a requirement that all applicants for employment by the state or any public school system be drug tested (*Georgia Ass'n of Educators v. Harris*, 749 F. Supp. 1110 (N.D. Ga. 1990)). A policy of making drug testing a condition of tenure has also been found to be unconstitutional (*Patchogue-Medford Congress of Teachers v. Board of Educ.*, 510 N.E.2d 325 (N.Y. 1987)).

It is clear that, where the employee's duties directly relate to the safety of students, mandatory routine drug testing will be upheld on the basis of the employee's Fourth Amendment rights being outweighed by the need for the institution to determine the fitness of the employee. This is based on long-standing Supreme Court law in noneducational contexts but has been applied to employees in the education setting, such as bus drivers, guards carrying weapons on school grounds, and, in at least one case, employees operating heavy machinery (Rapp 2012, §6.14). (Federal regulation mandates drug testing for school bus drivers.)

Some courts have held that school employees in safety-sensitive positions, including teachers, may be subject to mandatory drug testing without violation of their privacy rights if it can be shown that the testing is based on a legitimate concern about students' safety. (See, e.g., *Knox County Educ. Ass'n v. Knox*

County Bd. of Educ., 158 F.3d 361 (6th Cir. 1998); *Crager v. Board of Educ.*, 313 F. Supp. 2d 690 (E.D. Ky. 2004); *Jones v. Jenkins*, 878 F.2d 1476 (D.C. Cir. 1989).)

EMPLOYEE RIGHTS IN THE ELECTRONIC WORLD

The Stored Communications Act (SCA), discussed in Chapter 2, prohibits access to stored electronic communications but includes an exception for the entity providing the service. Thus, the SCA does not prohibit an employer from accessing stored emails if the email service is provided by the employer. This may be the case even if the computer accessed belongs to the employee. (See, e.g., *Soderstrand v. Oklahoma ex rel Bd. of Regents*, 463 F. Supp. 2d 1308 (W.D. Ok. 2006).)

In 2010, the Supreme Court explicitly recognized the danger of issuing broad holdings regarding the use of still-developing areas of technology:

> The judiciary risks error by elaborating too fully on the Fourth Amendment implications of emerging technology before its role in society has become clear. . . . Rapid changes in the dynamics of communication and information transmission are evident not just in the technology itself but in what society accepts as proper behavior. . . . At present, it is uncertain how workplace norms, and the law's treatment of them, will evolve. . . . [T]he Court would have difficulty predicting how employees' privacy expectations will be shaped by those changes or the degree to which society will be prepared to recognize those expectations as reasonable (*City of Ontario v. Quon*, 130 S. Ct. 2619, 2629–30 (2010) [citations omitted]).

In that case, the Ontario, California, Police Department issued pagers capable of sending and receiving text messages to all members of its S.W.A.T. team for the purpose of helping them mobilize and respond to emergencies. Employees were told, both verbally and in writing, that the city reserved the right to monitor all computer activity, including that of the pagers, and that employees should have no expectation of privacy in using such resources. The city's plan with a private service provider limited the amount of data sent and received each month. When Quon's use exceeded the limit, he was told that he could reimburse the city for the additional cost as an alternative to having his supervisor audit his messages to determine if the overage was due to work-related transmissions. Quon did this for several months. Eventually, the police chief decided to determine whether the current limit was too low to accommodate workplace needs. He ordered transcripts of the messages sent by Quon during the previous two months. The officer reviewing the transcripts first redacted all messages sent while Quon was off duty. In reviewing the messages sent while Quon was on duty, the officer found that only a minority were work-related. Quon was disciplined for violating departmental rules (*Id.*).

At trial, the Supreme Court applied the *New Jersey v. T.L.O.* reasonableness standard of inquiring into the reasonableness of the search at its inception and the reasonableness of its scope. It first declined to decide whether Quon had a reasonable expectation of privacy, expounding on the danger of establishing such a standard in the context of newly developing technology and changing social expectations related to that technology; instead, the Court proceeded on the basis of assuming arguendo that Quon had an expectation of privacy (*Id.* at 2629–30). However, the Court also noted that any expectation of privacy Quon might have was limited: He had been told that his messages could be audited; as a police officer, he should have known that his actions and workplace communications were likely to come under legal scrutiny; and he should have anticipated that the city would audit messages to assess the S.W.A.T. team's performance (*Id.* at 2631).

The Court held that the search was reasonable at its inception because the city had a legitimate interest in determining whether the data limit of the plan was sufficient to meet the city's needs. The Court disagreed with Quon's argument that the scope of the search was overly intrusive, noting that the city had obtained only two months' worth of transcripts and had redacted all off-duty messages before reviewing the transcripts (*Id.*).

EMPLOYEE'S RIGHT TO PRIVACY OUTSIDE OF THE WORK ENVIRONMENT

It is clearly established that employees of educational institutions may be disciplined or dismissed based on their activities and conduct in private life, when not on the job or at the workplace, only if the employee's conduct seriously and adversely affects the employee's ability to perform his or her job or otherwise negatively effects the ability of the institution to operate smoothly. "To overcome the privacy interest, a legitimate interest of the school board has to be at stake, that is, there must be additional evidence of a resulting unfavorable impact on the teacher's fitness to teach or upon the school community" (*Powell v. Paine*, 655 S.E.2d 204 (W.Va. 2007)). "[W]here his professional achievement is unaffected, where the school community is placed in no jeopardy, [a teacher's] private acts are his own business and may not be the basis of discipline" (*Jarvella v. Willoughby-Eastlake City Sch. Dist. Bd. of Educ.*, 233 N.E. 2d 143, 146 (Ohio C.P. 1967)). Even an employee's illegal conduct in his or her private life may not be sufficient to allow the institution to discipline the employee, unless it affects his or her ability to perform the job. Significant public reaction to the employee's actions may rise to the level of affecting the ability to perform his or her job (Rapp 2012,§6.10).

Privacy rights intersect with First Amendment rights to a significant degree in the context of disciplining employees based on nonwork activities, making it difficult to discuss one without the other in many cases. As a general rule, an institution may not limit an educational employee's participation in outside activities—including membership in certain groups—unless the activities adversely impact the employee's ability to perform his or her job (Rapp 2012, §6.14).

Not surprisingly, a majority of case law addressing this issue involves a teacher's or faculty member's sexual behavior. I will not address the issues of sexual interactions with students or sexual harassment, which involve their own major sets of legal issues—often criminal in nature—and relate to much more than privacy. Here, I discuss sexual behavior only from the perspective of an educational employee's right to privacy in his or her otherwise legal sexual behavior. The bottom line in any case is whether, or the degree to which, the behavior at issue affects the teacher's ability to be effective in his or her job. A comparison of some cases in which punishing an educational employee for his or her private sexual behavior has been allowed and others in which it has been held to violate the employee's privacy rights shows how fact-specific the analysis is.

Discipline or dismissal of educational employees has been upheld when an elementary school teacher cohabited with her boyfriend in a small, rural community where so much notoriety attached that it affected her ability to teach effectively (*Sullivan v. Meade Indep. Sch. Dist. No. 101*, 530 F.2d 799 (8th Cir. 1976)). In a small town, firing a sixth-grade teacher was upheld where the teacher, on his own property but in public view, undressed, caressed, and carried on in a lewd and suggestive manner with a mannequin (*Wishart v. McDonald*, 500 F.2d 1110 (1st Cir. 1974)). The Second Circuit acknowledged that a high school teacher's ability to associate with and advocate for the North American Man/Boy Love Association, a.k.a. NAMBLA, was protected by the First Amendment, but nonetheless upheld the teacher's dismissal, as the school board had succeeded in proving that the teacher's actions had disrupted the school's mission and would likely cause fear in the community (*Melzer v. Board of Educ.*, 336 F.3d 185 (2d Cir. 2003)).

In comparison, courts have overturned the dismissal of teachers of primary and secondary schools when the educational institution was unable to show that the sexual relationship at issue adversely affected the ability to teach in the following situations: a consensual sexual relationship outside of marriage (*Sherburne v. School Bd. of Suwannee County*, 455 So. 2d 1057 (Fla. Dist. Ct. App. 1984)); an adulterous affair (*Bertolini v. Whitehall City Sch. Dist. Bd. of Educ.*, 744 N.E.2d 1245 (2000)); and an affair with the parent of a student (*Gosche v. Calvert High Sch.*, 997 F. Supp. 867 (N.D. Ohio 1998)).

The same standard applies to instructors who are homosexual. Modern case law makes clear that homosexuality in and of itself is not sufficient to dismiss an instructor (Rapp 2012, §6.14).

In any case, however, the key issue is not the particular situation—e.g., a teacher engaged in an extramarital affair—but whether the action or situation affects the teacher's ability to perform his or her job.

BIBLIOGRAPHY

Bertolini v. Whitehall City Sch. Dist. Bd. of Educ., 744 N.E.2d 1245 (2000).

City of Ontario v. Quon, 130 S. Ct. 2619 (2010).

Crager v. Board of Educ., 313 F. Supp. 2d 690 (E.D. Ky. 2004).

Florida v. Riley, 488 U.S. 445 (1989).

Georgia Ass'n of Educators v. Harris, 749 F. Supp. 1110 (N.D. Ga. 1990).

Gillard v. Schmidt, 579 F.2d 825 (3d Cir. 1978).

Gosche v. Calvert High Sch., 997 F. Supp. 867 (N.D. Ohio 1998).

Jarvella v. Willoughby-Eastlake City Sch. Dist. Bd. of Educ., 233 N.E. 2d 143 (Ohio C.P. 1967).

Jones v. Jenkins, 878 F.2d 1476 (D.C. Cir. 1989).

Knox County Educ. Ass'n v. Knox County Bd. of Educ., 158 F.3d 361 (6th Cir. 1998).

Melzer v. Board of Educ., 336 F.3d 185 (2d Cir. 2003).

Nelson v. Salem State Coll., 845 N.E.2d 338 (Mass. 2006).

O'Connor v. Ortega, 480 U.S. 709 (1987).

Patchogue-Medford Congress of Teachers v. Board of Educ., 510 N.E.2d 325 (N.Y. 1987).

People v. Powell, 599 N.W.2d 499 (Mich. Ct. App. 1999).

Plock v. Board of Ed., 545 F. Supp. 2d 755 (N.D. Ill. 2007).

Powell v. Paine, 655 S.E.2d 204 (W. Va. 2007).

Rapp, James, *Education Law* (New York: Matthew Bender & Co. 2012).

Reno v. East Baton Rouge Parish Sch. Bd., 697 F. Supp. 2d 659 (M.D. La. 2010).

Schowengerdt v. General Dynamics Corp., 823 F.2d 1328 (9th Cir. 1987).

Shaul v. Cherry Valley-Springfield Cent. Sch. Dist., 363 F.3d 177 (2d Cir. 2004).

Sherburne v. School Bd. of Suwannee County, 455 So. 2d 1057 (Fla. Dist. Ct. App. 1984).

Soderstrand v. Oklahoma ex rel Bd. of Regents, 463 F. Supp. 2d 1308 (W.D. Ok. 2006).

Sullivan v. Meade Indep. Sch. Dist. No. 101, 530 F.2d 799 (8th Cir. 1976).

United States v. Buettner-Janusch, 646 F.2d 759 (2d Cir. 1981).

United Teachers of New Orleans v. Orleans Parish Sch. Bd., 142 F.3d 853 (5th Cir. 1998).

Watkins v. L. M. Berry & Co., 704 F.2d 577 (11th Cir. 1983).

Wishart v. McDonald, 500 F.2d 1110 (1st Cir. 1974).

PART III

Moving Forward

CHAPTER 8

Privacy Policies

Students, parents and teachers alike would be well served if school boards, after full public discussion, adopted carefully drawn regulations defining when, where, by whom and under what circumstances searches of students may be conducted. Such regulations would go far in determining the community's view of "reasonable conduct" and would stand the best chance of reconciling the student's legitimate privacy interests with the educational necessities of the school environment (*D.R.C. v. State*, 646 P.2d 252, 261 (Alaska Ct. App. 1982)).

Written policies serve a variety of valuable purposes. Simply the process of writing a policy can bring together different segments of the community, including students, parents, administration, and law enforcement; help all parties narrow and articulate their goals and expectations; and generate community support. The policy itself serves the purposes of clarifying expectations and rules, ensuring consistent procedures, and educating the community.

Policies can be particularly valuable when addressing issues on which the law is silent or conflicting, as is true for many areas in which privacy concerns are greatest, primarily regarding new and evolving technologies. However, policies must be written in the context of existing law. It is imperative that your policy not contradict the law governing your institution or conflict with other institutional policies. In addition, your policy must take into account the particular needs and characteristics of your institution. This is why it is so important to involve your institution's legal counsel in the process.

Policies can also be helpful in clarifying in what situations students and staff should have a reasonable expectation of privacy. Courts have referred to the implementation of an institution's policy in determining whether a student's expectations of privacy in the given circumstance are reasonable. For example, if the policy states that the school may inspect lockers at any time, for any reason, without giving prior notice, a student cannot then claim a reasonable expectation of privacy in the contents of his or her locker. (See, e.g., *Zamora v. Pomeroy*, 639 F.2d 662 (10th Cir. 1981).) However, this is true only for situations in which the institution may have a right to invade the individual's privacy. Under some circumstances, a person's reasonable expectation of privacy can never be eliminated; in such cases, a statement otherwise in a policy will not be given any weight by the court. In *Doe v. Little Rock School District*, for example, the statement in the student handbook that if a student's personal containers such as book bags and purses were "brought onto school property, such containers and their contents are at all times subject to random and periodic inspections by school officials" did not override the unconstitutionality of random, suspicionless, generalized searches of students' possessions (*Doe v. Little Rock Sch. Dist.*, 380 F.3d 349, 354 (8th Cir. 2004)). Note that the court distinguished the role that might be played by such a policy regarding the belongings of faculty and staff: "The students are required by state law to attend school, and have not entered into a contract that incorporates the handbook or voluntarily assented to be bound by its terms. The lack of mutual consent to the student handbook makes it fundamentally different from an employee handbook, which may create an enforceable contract between an employer and employee under traditional contract principles" (*Id.*).

Because one of the most valuable roles of a policy is ensuring consistency in practices, your privacy policy ideally should be issued at the highest administrative level, so that the same policy will apply to all schools in the district and, to the degree appropriate, to all campuses within a college or university system. Even if your administration prefers to have different privacy policies for different institutions, the administration should be involved in creating the policy from the beginning. It is not strictly necessary for a member or members of the administration to participate in the actual drafting of the policy, but the administration is responsible for setting the approach the policy will take. As you have seen throughout this book, the law regarding privacy rights is often situation-specific, which provides a certain amount of flexibility in how you approach defining your policies. An institution that is challenged by high levels of drug use or violence may choose to be more restrictive of student privacy rights, whereas an institution with very few serious problems may choose to provide students with a higher level of privacy protection. In the former case, the institution will probably want to have the right to search student lockers, perhaps without notice. Its policy should state that it has the right to do so; if not, it opens up the possibility for a student to argue that he or she has a reasonable expectation of privacy in the items the student keeps in his or her locker, such that the institution cannot search it without giving prior notice. This is not to imply that the argument will succeed, but omitting a provision giving the institution the right to search creates a degree of ambiguity.

The following discussion addresses writing "a privacy policy." In reality, privacy is implicated in so many practices of an educational institution that it is likely addressed in multiple policies for other areas. For example, the institution's Acceptable Use Policy for use of computers likely addresses some privacy issues, and a policy on bullying or harassment would have privacy implications, even if not specifically addressed in the policy. In addition, privacy policies should provide guidelines for faculty and staff practices as well as student practices; it may or may not be appropriate to address both in the same document. Your institution may decide to have a single privacy policy that includes all its statements regarding privacy, to address privacy issues where pertinent in already existing policies, or some combination of the two. Regardless of the final format, the following should provide helpful guidelines.

For public K–12 schools, many state school board associations provide model policies, and some districts may require the use of these policies, either as guidelines to writing a tailored policy or to be used without modification as the district's policy.

STEPS IN WRITING A PRIVACY POLICY

Consider Who to Include in the Process

This is a good opportunity for finding or creating consensus within the broader community and for all interested parties to come to understand each other's needs and concerns. Consider whether it would be valuable for your community to include parents, students, law enforcement, and any other group with a relationship with the school, and what role they will play in the process. How will you solicit and obtain their input? Do you want the committee writing the policy to include members from each constituency? Would you prefer to have only school staff involved in the writing, but hold open meetings during the process? Whatever process you choose, be sure to clarify who will make final decisions regarding creation and implementation of the policy. At the minimum, representatives from administration, instructors, librarians, and counselors should be involved.

It is imperative that your institution's legal counsel be included as much as possible in the process of writing and implementing your policy. Your policy will be addressing and interpreting legal issues, both directly and indirectly. As this book makes clear, privacy law is complex and complicated, and sometimes even contradictory. Your legal counsel needs to be included to ensure that your policy abides by all applicable law. If your counsel is not a privacy expert or does not feel comfortable advising the district on privacy at such a detailed level, he or she should be able to identify and work with an attorney with expertise in the area of privacy law.

Identify the Areas to Be Addressed by the Policy; Specify Conditions

List the situations or issues that your policy needs to address, without yet deciding what position you will take. Common situations include searching of student lockers, backpacks, and cars; monitoring student use of the Internet; access to student school Internet accounts; access to student nonschool accounts when the student is using them on school equipment; access to content stored on electronic devices owned by the student; monitoring physical spaces on institutional grounds; monitoring residential areas; privacy of student records retained by the school and district, including library records; and drug testing.

In creating this list, identify any situations that have caused difficulty, problems, or confusion in the past. All of these situations need to go on your list.

Review Current Policies and Consider Current and Past Practices

What do existing policies say about privacy? Does current practice comport with existing policies? What situations have occurred that are not addressed in current policies? How have these situations been addressed in the past? Is the practice consistent among schools within the district or system? What has been successful, and what has not? Do you need to take different approaches in different situations, perhaps depending on the level or age of the student?

Conduct a privacy audit of information collected, maintained, and used by the institution: Be sure that you know what type of data your institution collects about employees as well as students, how they are stored and for how long, and who has access to them. Articulate the purpose for which the data is collected. You should be collecting no more data than is necessary, and retaining it for no longer than necessary (which may be dictated by law). Access and use should be restricted to only those who need to access and use the data; the more sensitive the information, the tighter the restrictions should be, generally speaking. Specify these details in your policy.

Content

Review applicable state and federal laws. Work with legal counsel to be confident that you know how they apply to the situations you have identified.

Do not simply state the law addressing a certain issue as the entirety of the section on that issue. Keeping in mind that the policy must be user-friendly to be useful, quote from the law only when it helps the user to understand the point. Alternatively, you may refer to the law, and direct the user to it.

Structure applicable parts of your policy around the Fair Information Practices discussed in Chapter 1. These practices articulate an international consensus on the approach to respecting individual privacy rights.

For primary and secondary institutions, even though the Children's Online Privacy Protection Act applies only to commercial websites, aligning your policy with its requirements regarding collection of online information is a good approach to take. Both parents and minors are familiar with these provisions and may have come to expect them; and the Federal Trade Commission, which oversees COPPA, strongly encourages schools to adopt its approach.

Address in specific, unambiguous terms the situations you have identified. Consider and address exceptions to restrictions. For example, note that records will be turned over when required by court order. Explain any other circumstances in which you will provide information when not definitively required by law; for example, will you turn over records in response to a subpoena? Are there certain circumstances in which you will notify parents of a student's behavior?

The policy should specify under what conditions and in what situations it applies, and note any differences defined by the context. For example, the policy might specify that it applies to students within a particular zone of the institution's grounds, or to any school-sponsored events or activities, regardless of location. If you decide to implement different policies for different ages or grade levels of students, state that. For example, you may establish a drug-testing program for athletes only at the senior high school level.

Residential schools, whether postsecondary or K–12, should address searches of dorm rooms and other living quarters.

Explain how the policy will be enforced. If you plan to involve law enforcement in particular circumstances, note this.

Include contact information for the person or people who can answer questions about the policy.

Final Reviews

Compare what you have just written with existing policies. Be sure they are consistent. If not, explore why they vary so that you can determine the most accurate and appropriate approach.

Be sure your legal counsel reviews and approves the draft. Your policies are legal documents; none should be implemented until you receive final approval from your institution's legal counsel.

When you have finalized your draft policy, take it back to the community identified in the first step of the process. Provide an appropriate amount of time to receive feedback, and amend the policy as deemed necessary. If you make substantive amendments, send it back to your legal counsel for approval of the changes.

WHAT TO DO WITH YOUR PRIVACY POLICY

A policy itself is only a piece of paper. It is a tool, whose value lies in how it is used. Disseminate your policy widely, to all who need to know about it. At the minimum, this should include faculty, staff, and administrators, students, and parents. Determine the most effective manner in which to distribute the policy. You should include the policy in any manuals for students, faculty, and staff, and include it on institutional websites.

Consider how your privacy policy intersects with other district policies. Be sure that your policies do not contradict each other. You may also need to decide how to incorporate your policies with each other, such as whether your Acceptable Use Policy should refer to your privacy policy rather than address the same issue in both policies.

Provide training to faculty, staff, and administrators. Where appropriate, include it in student orientation. The ultimate goal of the training is to ensure that everyone clearly understands the policy so that it will be carried out consistently across the district or system.

Determine a schedule for conducting audits to confirm that the policy is being implemented consistently and to identify and address any problems. Establish a process for updating the policy as needed, including how to track changes in law that would require amendments to the policy.

GENERAL TIPS FOR WRITING A PRIVACY POLICY

As is true for any policy to be useful, the policy must be specific enough to avoid ambiguities. For example, a policy that prohibits student possession of "drugs" is open to interpretation: Is the term "drugs" meant to refer only to illicit drugs? Does it include all prescription drugs? Only prescription drugs for which the student does not have a prescription? Or is it meant to be extremely broad and refer also to any over-the-counter medications? Even then, there could be room for ambiguity: Would prohibiting all over-the-counter medications refer only to those consumed orally, or also to topical medications such as antibiotic salves? A policy does not need to include a laundry list of prohibited items so long as the language is clear enough to be easily understood and leaves no room for ambiguity.

The policy must be user-friendly enough to be useful. A policy that is not implemented is worthless, if not harmful; and a policy that does not make sense to its audience is very difficult to implement. Your policy should be useful for faculty, staff, and administration, students, and parents. Writing a policy that is user-friendly for all these audiences can be tricky; discuss how you will address any challenges. You might want to consider writing a dual-layered policy. The first layer is essentially an executive summary. It may lay out the terms of the policy in general statements, with references to the full policy.

BIBLIOGRAPHY

Doe ex r. Doe v. Little Rock Sch. Dist., 380 F.3d 349 (8th Cir. 2004).
D.R.C. v. State, 646 P.2d 252 (Alaska Ct. App. 1982).
Zamora v. Pomeroy, 639 F.2d 662 (10th Cir. 1981).

CHAPTER 9

Privacy in a Digital Future: Protecting Our Institutions and Our Students

EMERGING TECHNOLOGIES AND THE STATE OF PRIVACY LAW

What Is a Reasonable Expectation of Privacy in the World of Evolving Technology?

Privacy rights are based on a "reasonable expectation of privacy." A person has a reasonable expectation of privacy when he or she has "exhibited an actual (subjective) expectation of privacy and . . . the expectation [is] one that society is prepared to recognize as 'reasonable'" (*Katz v. United States*, 389 U.S. 347, 361 (1967)). It has been long established that items "in plain view" cannot be subject to a reasonable expectation of privacy. (See, e.g., *id*.) The Supreme Court has explained the plain view doctrine thus:

> [A] man's home is, for most purposes, a place where he expects privacy, but objects, activities, or statements that he exposes to the "plain view" of outsiders are not "protected" because no intention to keep them to himself has been exhibited. On the other hand, conversations in the open would not be protected against being overheard, for the expectation of privacy under the circumstances would be unreasonable (*Id*. [citations omitted]).

Early jurisprudence tied the reasonableness of an expectation of privacy to physical place. In a 1928 case, the Court upheld the government's wiretapping of phone lines leading into the plaintiff's house because "there was no entry of the houses . . ." (*Olmstead v. United States*, 277 U.S. 438 (1928)). As technology evolved, so did the Court's interpretation of Fourth Amendment protection. Almost 40 years later, the Court expressly stated that the underpinnings of the *Olmstead* case had been "eroded" over time and were no longer controlling when it found unconstitutional the wiretapping without warrant of a public telephone booth, despite the fact that clearly there was no physical intrusion on private property.

> For the Fourth Amendment protects people, not places. What a person knowingly exposes to the public, even in his own home or office, is not a subject of Fourth Amendment protection. But what he seeks to preserve

as private, even in an area accessible to the public, may be constitutionally protected (*Katz*, 389 U.S. at 351).

In previous chapters, we have seen cases dealing with privacy in a digital "place," such as *R.S. v. Minnewaska Area School District*, in which a district court found a reasonable expectation of privacy in a student's private Facebook postings and email (*R.S. v. Minnewaska Area Sch. Dist.*, 2012 U.S. Dist. LEXIS 126257 (D. Minn. 2012)). At least one court has held that the ability of cell phones "to store large amounts of private data gives their users a reasonable and justifiable expectation of a higher level of privacy in the information they contain" than in nonelectronic devices (*State of Ohio v. Smith*, 920 N.E.2d 949, 955 (Ohio 2009)). However, applying the law to the changing nature of our physical things that allow us to store vast amounts of personal data and information remains a very unsettled issue.

What Standard Should Determine the Reasonableness of Fourth Amendment Searches and Seizures in a Digital World?

The standard articulated by the Supreme Court in *New Jersey v. T.LO.* remains the standard for determining whether the invasion of a student's privacy by an educational institution is constitutional, regardless of the technology involved. Increasingly, however, legal scholars and privacy advocates are questioning the applicability of this standard to situations involving modern technology. (See, e.g., Hirsch 2011; Spung 2011.) Chapter 6 discussed this issue in the context of cell phones and the massive amounts of data stored in them. As technology continues to evolve, these issues will continue to grow.

As noted above, some courts have begun to recognize a reasonable expectation for a higher level of privacy in personal electronic devices, such as cell phones and laptops, than in traditional containers, such as lockers and backpacks. In the criminal context, this has led courts to apply a higher standard for determining the reasonableness of a search. Under criminal law, law enforcement officers may make warrantless searches in certain situations, such as in connection with an arrest. However, even when the search of a person and his or her effects in connection with an arrest is constitutional, some courts have held that police must meet the higher standard of obtaining a warrant before searching the contents of personal electronic devices found in the search (*State of Ohio v. Smith*, 920 N.E.2d 949).

Nonetheless, the courts remain conflicted in this area. Even in the criminal context, in which a significant and robust body of Fourth Amendment case law has developed, courts disagree over whether a constitutional search of a vehicle and the closed containers in that vehicle should extend to a search of the contents of cell phones, laptops, and other electronic devices found in the vehicle. As I write, Congress is considering legislation that would require a warrant to engage in such searches, but the future of that legislation is not clear.

Of course, the Fourth Amendment applies only to searches and seizures by government officials, although much state tort law, applicable to private entities and individuals, applies the same principles. In the private realm, companies who make a business out of digital information may themselves be conflicted in their attitudes toward the protection of consumer data and information. On the one hand, these companies know that their users need some level of assurance that their privacy will be protected before users will engage the companies' services or products. On the other hand, many of these companies make money from collecting, using, and even sharing user data, such as using it for targeted advertising or improving their products. Regardless of how their position on any given issue or piece of legislation, these entities are actively involved in legislative issues that affect their businesses.

More squarely representing user rights in the legislative arena, organizations such as the Electronic Frontier Foundation, the Electronic Privacy Information Center, and the Center for Democracy and Technology monitor and advocate for legislation that will unambiguously protect the privacy of users. They too, however, realize that too much restriction on use of data will squelch the growth of technology and the economy, which of course significantly impacts the information users whose privacy they seek to protect.

The law and standards that determine how we define a reasonable expectation of privacy and that address privacy issues in connection with still evolving technologies must evolve as technology does so. Because the law will always lag behind, as we are now seeing, it is more important than ever for educational institutions to be proactive in educating themselves about the privacy implications of new technologies, creating informed policies appropriate for the needs of their institutions and their students, and educating their communities accordingly.

EMERGING TECHNOLOGIES IN THE EDUCATION CONTEXT

Of the various evolving technologies currently being embraced by educational institutions at all levels, cloud computing, social media, and location tracking are perhaps those most rapidly being adopted. All three carry extreme risks in the context of data security and privacy protection, and yet little if any law addresses these particular technologies, leaving the vendor contract as the only avenue for protection. Further, the institutions adopting them so quickly often fail to give adequate consideration to these issues.

The Cloud

References to "cloud computing," or simply "the cloud," have become commonplace. But what exactly is "the cloud"? At its most basic level, cloud computing refers to storing your data on someone else's server. Thus, the cloud can be used for any type of computing function traditionally conducted on a computer located on your institution's grounds. When you use Outlook or a similar program for email, the program has been loaded onto your institution's system, and all of the information you store in the email program—emails, contacts, calendars, task lists—physically resides on your (or your institution's) device. In comparison, when you use Gmail, Yahoo Mail, or other Internet-based services for your email, your information resides on Google's or Yahoo's servers; your information is in the cloud.

An increasing variety of cloud-based services are being offered, and an increasing number of entities are turning to cloud services to replace their more traditional modes of computing, including educational entities (Solove 2012). As with anything, cloud computing offers both benefits and risks.

For many institutions, using the cloud for records storage or communication services can significantly cut costs. Your institution does not have to purchase, update, or maintain a computing system, or hire information technology specialists to do so. With increasingly sophisticated technology, a cloud computing service may be able to provide greater expertise and even greater security than can your institution. Cloud computing can also make working collaboratively much easier, as multiple individuals can have simultaneous access to the same version of a document.

However, because the data storage is beyond your institution's physical control, you lose some amount of control over the data itself. It is common for cloud companies to outsource data storage, often with the result that the data resides on a server in a different country with entirely different—if any—privacy and other laws protecting that data. More specifically, the laws of some countries where cloud storage is frequently located, such as China and India, specifically allow the mining and sale of data.

As of the time of this writing, no U.S. laws specifically address cloud computing. Recall that the Electronic Communications Privacy Act (ECPA) cobbles together different types and degrees of protection for electronic data, depending on the medium of the data. Attempts to revise the ECPA began in 2010 and encountered various walls. In November 2012, Senator Patrick Leahy, chair of the Senate Jurisprudence Committee, introduced legislation that would allow over 20 federal agencies to access email, documents stored in the cloud, and social media postings without first obtaining a search warrant. In some cases, it would also allow the FBI and the Department of Homeland Security to obtain complete access to Internet user accounts with absolutely no prior warning or judicial oversight at all—the agencies could do so without notifying either the user or even a court (McCollagh 2012).

Until new legislation is passed, educational institutions must rely on what they know of law written for older technologies. For example, FERPA's protections for educational records apply to records in any medium. The educational institution is ultimately responsible for what happens to those records; outsourcing storage or processing does not outsource responsibility.

It is imperative that you do your due diligence in selecting a cloud service provider. As with any contract, you should consult your institution's legal counsel before engaging a cloud service provider. If your legal counsel is not familiar with the context of cloud computing, be sure to educate him or her regarding both the benefits and the risks. The National Institute of Standards and Technology, within the U.S. Commerce Department, has issued a thorough set of guidelines to assist in selecting a cloud service provider. These guidelines describe "the threats, technology risks, and safeguards surrounding public cloud environments, and their treatment," and provide a valuable tool in selecting an appropriate cloud service provider (National Institute of Standards and Technology 2011). Many other, less stringent, guidelines are available to help you in assessing a safe service.

Social Media

As discussed in Chapters 5 and 6, it would seem that the Fourth Amendment protects against unreasonable searches and seizures by government officials of much information shared via social media. This assumes, however, that the user has made attempts to limit access to the information or otherwise indicate that he or she has an expectation of privacy.

Legislation addressing privacy rights in social media against both government and private parties has been slow to develop. Legislators often respond to pressure from their constituents. In recent years, the media gave much attention to employers' use of social media to investigate applicants for employment. Much of the public felt uneasy about this, as we often consider our use of social media to be part of our private lives; indeed, the very reason potential employers jump on social media for this purpose is because it allows them to discover information about potential employees that they would never have learned in the brick-and-mortar world without hiring a private detective. The straw that broke the camel's back, however, was a flood of stories about potential employers demanding from job applicants login information and passwords for social media accounts. Not long after this practice came to public attention, states—not Congress—began to pass legislation regulating such activities.

Some have gone further and prohibited educational institutions from engaging in the same and similar activities, not waiting for courts to confirm that such demands would be found unconstitutional. As the tool of social media becomes more widely used in educational settings—not only for personal reasons but as a tool for education—absent specific laws addressing the topic, educators should be guided by the *T.L.O.* standard and their own institution's policies.

Location Tracking Technology

For the past decade, schools at all levels have experimented with the use of location tracking devices embedded in student identification cards or other items carried or worn by students. These devices are capable of tracking a student's location with near pinpoint precision, transmitting that data to remote locations, and retaining records of the data. Much of this work is outsourced, with the result being that private companies have control over the information collected. In the absence of law, the degree to which the privacy of that data—and thus the students to whom it relates—is protected is controlled solely by contract. Not surprisingly, these situations have raised serious privacy (and other) concerns.

In 2012, the Supreme Court held unconstitutional law enforcement's placing of a GPS tracking device on a criminal suspect's car (*United States v. Jones*, 132 S. Ct. 945 (2012)). However, its holding was based in large part on the fact that law enforcement had entered the suspect's private property—his driveway —to do so. The Court was careful to distinguish cases in which it allowed the use of beepers to track the location of suspects when the actual act of planting the beeper had not invaded the suspect's privacy. Although all justices agreed with the unconstitutional nature of planting the GPS device, their analyses differed dramatically. Four justices criticized the majority opinion for "present [ing] particularly vexing problems" in cases that do not involve physical contact, such as "those that involve the transmission of electronic signals." In response, the majority succinctly stated, "Situations involving merely the transmission of electronic signals without trespass would remain subject to *Katz* analysis" (*Id.* at 953).

Given that the *Katz* Court emphasized the Fourth Amendment's protection of people, not places, that statement should be comforting. However, the fact that four justices were so greatly disturbed by the analysis of the majority opinion suggests that how *Katz* will be applied in purely electronic situations is far from clear.

Meanwhile, educational institutions move ahead with implementing the use of a variety of location tracking mechanisms, from embedding Radio Frequency Identification (RFID) chips in the clothing of preschoolers (Ozer 2010) to requiring older students to carry with them at all times student ID cards tracking their every move (Associated Press 2012). Being able to constantly and instantaneously track student location increases both student safety and institutional efficiency, and is ultimately cost-saving, according to the various institutions implementing such technologies. They are used for purposes such as replacing manual attendance records; tracking a student's movements at school and on field trips, presumably for security purposes; and collecting data such as whether a child has eaten that day (Associated Press 2012, Ozer 2010).

Since the practice began, at least as early as 2005, however, privacy watch-dogs and children's advocates have raised warnings, citing both the vulnerability of RFID technology and a lack of transparency regarding what data is collected, how long it is retained, and who has access to the information. (See, e.g., Electronic Frontier Foundation 2010; Hirsch 2011.) Critics point not only to privacy concerns but also to security of the students themselves, relying on a wealth of experiments and studies exposing the ease with which RFID technology can be hacked and the data stolen or even duplicated. (See, e.g., Hirsch 2011.) At least one court may soon have the chance to rule on these uses; the family of a high school student in San Antonio, Texas, has filed suit over their daughter's expulsion from school for refusing to wear the newly mandated "smart ID." However, the claim in that case is infringement of religious freedom, not privacy. Nonetheless, civil rights groups have rallied around the lawsuit, hoping that it will bring greater attention to the issue (Associated Press 2012).

THE CRYSTAL BALL OF PRIVACY RIGHTS

What does the future hold regarding the privacy rights of students, faculty and staff, and others in the educational setting? Both Congress and states continue to debate these issues and draft legislation, sometimes succeeding in passing it. Some legislation promotes the protection of individual privacy rights; other legislation sits on the other side of the scale, tipping it towards the ability of government or other third parties to access, collect, and use personal information. Meanwhile, a growing number of legal scholars and privacy advocates are calling for a higher standard than the *T.L.O.* reasonableness standard to be applied in the educational context when dealing with online information and electronic devices. (See, e.g., Hirsch 2011; Spung 2011.)

Although it is not clear where we are heading, what is clear is that where the law is silent or conflicting, protection of privacy is, at best, uncertain. This leaves the user of information technology in the position of being his or her own protector.

BIBLIOGRAPHY

Associated Press, "Track Suit: Family Challenges 'Locator' Chips Embedded in Student ID Cards at Texas Schools," http://www.washingtonpost.com/national/on-faith/track-suit-family-challenges-locator-chips-embedded-in-student-id-cards-at-texas-schools/2012/11/27/7ce93a3a-38e0-11e2-9258-ac7c78d5c680_story.html (November 27, 2012).

Cornell University Information Technologies, "Outsourcing and Cloud Computing for Higher Education," http://www.it.cornell.edu/cms/policies/cloud/index.cfm (cited December 4, 2012).

Electronic Frontier Foundation, "Privacy and Safety Questions Loom Over Federal Program to Track Preschoolers," https://www.eff.org/press/archives/2010/09/13 (September 14, 2010).

Hirsch, Alexandra C., "Schools: Where Fewer Rights Are Reasonable? Why the Reasonableness Standard Is Inappropriate to Measure the Use of RFID Tracking Devices on Students," 28 *J. Marshall J. Computer & Info. L.* 411 (2011).

Katz v. United States, 389 U.S. 347, 361 (1967).

McCollagh, Declan, "Senate Bill Rewrite Lets Feds Read Your E-mail without Warrants," http://news.cnet.com/8301-13578_3-57552225-38/senate-bill-rewrite-lets-feds-read-your-e-mail-without-warrants/?part=rss&subj=news&tag=title (November 20, 2012).

National Institute of Standards and Technology, "Guidelines on Security and Privacy in Public Cloud Computing," http://www.nist.gov/customcf/get_pdf.cfm?pub_id=909494 (December 2011).

Olmstead v. United States, 277 U.S. 438 (1928).

Ozer, Nicole, "Don't Let Schools Chip Your Kids," http://www.aclu.org/blog/content/dont-let-schools-chip-your-kids (September 1, 2010).

R.S. v. Minnewaska Area School District, 2012 U.S. Dist. LEXIS 126257 (Dist. Minn. 2012).

Solove, Daniel J., "Educational Institutions and Cloud Computing: A Roadmap of Responsibilities," http://www.huffingtonpost.com/daniel-j-solove/educational-institutions-_b_2156612.html (November 18, 2012).

Spung, A. James, "Comment: From Backpacks to BlackBerries: (Re)Examining *New Jersey v. T.L.O.* in the Age of the Cell Phone," 61 *Emory L. J.* 111 (2011).

State of Ohio v. Smith, 920 N.E.2d 949, 955 (Ohio 2009).

United States v. Jones, 132 S. Ct. 945 (2012).

CHAPTER 10

Quick and Dirty Answers

The following questions and answers are intended to serve as a quick reference resource in response to some of the most frequently asked questions about privacy in the educational setting. The brief answers should be considered a starting point to answering the questions, not an end point. Each answer lists the chapter(s) in which the issue(s) raised by the question is addressed in more detail.

Keep in mind all the caveats that have been raised throughout this book, however. The answer to your specific question will depend on the current law effective in your state and the details of your specific situation, which is why such "quick" answers are necessarily "dirty." If it were possible for such brief answers to solve all the issues raised in the following questions, there would be no need for this book or other resources like it! You should always consult your institution's legal counsel before making decisions about how to proceed in response to the situations raised by the following questions. As with all information provided in this book, do not consider the answers to these questions to constitute legal advice.

Which U.S. law governs privacy rights at the federal level?

No single statute in U.S. law governs privacy, and no one law broadly addresses privacy rights in general. Instead, U.S. privacy law is made up of a patchwork of both federal and state statutory laws that address privacy issues in specific situations, or that address broader issues in a certain situation, of which privacy happens to be only one. It can be complicated and sometimes confusing to piece together all of the laws applicable to any given situation. Furthermore, some state laws completely contradict the laws of other states, and sometimes state and federal laws even contradict each other. Your institution's legal counsel is the person to help you figure out which laws apply to you and what you need to know for a given situation. Chapters 1, 2, and 3.

My institution doesn't have a legal counsel. To whom do I turn for answers?

Every educational institution will have a legal counsel in some capacity. Academic institutions are more likely to have someone "in house," or as a full-time employee. For primary and secondary schools, the legal counsel may be an outside law firm with whom the school district contracts to provide legal services. In smaller communities, that may even be at the municipal level. Not all of these attorneys will be experts in privacy law, but if questions arise that they feel are beyond their expertise, they will help your institution find the appropriate expert in the area (such as privacy).

I know my institution has legal counsel, but I'm not allowed to contact him or her directly. What do I do?

When a situation arises in which it is important for you to know and understand privacy law, or receive legal advice in any way, or in which you encounter any kind of challenge involving the law, it is imperative that your institution's legal counsel be involved in deciding how the matter should be addressed. In such a situation, you should pass the matter "up the ladder" to your supervisor so that ultimately it reaches the legal counsel.

Which institutions MUST abide by FERPA, the Family Educational Rights and Privacy Act?

Any institution receiving funds from any program administered by the U.S. Department of Education is subject to loss of some or all of that funding if it does not abide by the requirements of FERPA. Almost all educational institutions, from pre-K through academia, and including private as well as public, receive some funds from the Department of Education and are thus subject to FERPA. Chapter 2.

Are schools subject to COPPA, the Children's Online Privacy Protection Act?

COPPA specifically regulates the operators of commercial websites, so most educational institutions will be exempt from its coverage. However, because its application is otherwise becoming so universal for websites created for children under the age of 13, parental and societal expectations are shaping themselves around COPPA's requirements. This is a good reason to take COPPA into account in designing websites or pages directed towards young students. Furthermore, the COPPA regulations simply serve as a good statement of best practices in providing websites directed towards young children. Chapter 2.

How does the U.S. Constitution apply to educational institutions?

The U.S. Constitution regulates the actions of both state and federal governmental entities. Public educational institutions at all levels constitute governmental entities, and their employees will be considered governmental officials in that capacity. Thus, the Constitution applies to the actions of all public educational institutions. Chapter 3.

When may an institution's officials search a particular student's belongings for contraband?

A search of a student's belongings must be "reasonable," based on the totality of the circumstances, both at its inception and in its scope. A search will be reasonable at its inception if the student voluntarily consents to the search or reasonable grounds exist for a suspicion that the student has violated either the rules of the educational institution or the law.

The scope of a search will be reasonable if the manner and degree of the search are reasonably related to the purpose of the search and the search is not more intrusive than necessary in light of the age and gender of the student and the nature of the alleged wrongdoing. The less serious or threatening the alleged wrong, the less intrusive the search may be. Chapter 5.

In which circumstances may an institution's officials search a particular student's person?

A search of a student himself or herself must be "reasonable," based on the totality of the circumstances, both at its inception and in its scope. Note, however, that searches of a student's person, such as via a pat-down, will often be considered more invasive than searching belongings. "Strip" searches, in which a student is asked or required to remove articles of clothing other than outerwear (such as a jacket), are considered quite invasive; thus, an institution should consult its legal counsel before engaging in strip searches or establishing policies allowing strip searches.

A search will be reasonable at its inception if the student voluntarily consents to the search, the institution's policies provide notice to the student of such a search, or reasonable grounds exist for a suspicion that the student has violated either the rules of the educational institution or the law. The scope of a search will be reasonable if the manner and degree of the search are reasonably related to the purpose of the search and the search is not more intrusive than necessary in light of the age and gender of the student and the nature of the alleged wrongdoing. The less serious or threatening the alleged wrong, the less intrusive the search may be. Chapter 5.

When may an institution's officials search the belongings of a group of students, such as conducting random classroom searches or searching students as they enter a building?

"Suspicionless" searches for the purpose of general security or safety, rather than searches based on the reasonable suspicion that an individual student is violating institutional policy or the law, should be limited in scope. Courts have upheld "generalized" searches of the student body that are minimally invasive, such as the use of metal detectors at the entrance to institutional grounds. A more invasive search should not be made of a group of students or their belongings unless reasonable grounds of suspicion exist of a threatening violation, and the institution does not have individual suspects. An example would be if the institution received a reliable warning that an unidentified student had carried a weapon onto campus. Even in such circumstances, the search should be as targeted at possible, based on the available knowledge. Chapter 5.

When may officials search the contents of student belongings containing personal information, such as diaries, letters, cell phones, or personal computers?

Because these types of items potentially contain very personal information, papers such as letters, diaries, or address books should be searched only if reason specifically exists to suspect that those items would reveal information related to that student's violation of the institution's policy or the law. The law is very unsettled regarding the searching of personal electronic devices, because they contain such large quantities of personal information and it is extremely difficult, if possible at all, to separate out the pieces that may be applicable to the purpose of the search. Ideally, institutions should not search personal electronic devices of students unless the institution's policies so allow; the institution's legal counsel should be heavily involved in creating such policies, and officials should abide carefully by the limitations of the policies. Chapters 5 and 6.

May educational institutions mandate drug testing of students?

Educational institutions may use mandatory drug testing of students involved in extracurricular activities, if the testing is targeted specifically at detecting the use of substances banned by the educational institution and the procedures of the testing ensure the privacy of the student's body during the testing process and the confidentiality of the results. Educational institutions generally may not use mandatory drug testing for the general student population, whether for all students or random selections of students. Chapter 5.

May educational institutions mandate drug tests for individual students suspected of using drugs?

Yes, if the reasonableness requirements of a search are met: The testing must be justified at its inception, meaning that the institution must have reasonable grounds for suspecting that the test will result in evidence of the student's drug use in violation of the institution's policy; and it must be reasonable in scope, meaning that the test should not be any more invasive than necessary to achieve that purpose. Both the testing process and the handling of the results should protect the student's privacy. Note that the suspicion of a student's drug use should be related to his or her behavior or performance at the educational institution; for example, a student should not be mandatorily tested for drugs based on information that he or she used drugs at a party over the weekend if his or her behavior or performance at school is not at issue. Chapter 5.

When may an educational institution search on-campus student residences?

Private institutions are not subject to constitutional restrictions on searches. Officials of public institutions may search on-campus student residences without obtaining prior permission in the case of individualized suspicion if the search meets the *T.L.O.* reasonableness standard. An institution wanting to engage in generalized searches without obtaining prior permission should first consult with its legal counsel, as limitations on the search will be determined based on the circumstances. Chapter 5.

May educational institutions use drug-sniffing dogs?

Courts generally agree that drug dogs can be used to search unopened student possessions when the dog is well trained and handled by a professional. If the dog alerts on an item, it may then be opened and searched. Courts disagree, however, on the constitutionality of using drug dogs to search students themselves. Chapter 5.

What areas may an educational institution monitor remotely? When may recordings be made?

Absent state law to the contrary, areas where students would not have a reasonable expectation of privacy—namely public areas such as hallways, classrooms, and open outdoor areas—may be monitored and recorded by silent video. In areas in which a student would have a reasonable expectation of privacy, such as a locker room, the *T.L.O.* standard must be met.

Most states have laws regulating the video, audio, and/or audiovisual monitoring and recording of others. These laws differ dramatically from state to state. Thus, any institution—whether private or public—should consult with its legal counsel before instigating a surveillance program. Chapter 5.

May an educational institution monitor or track students' online activity while the students are on institutional property?

Monitoring students' online activity, just as monitoring their reading habits, can have a chilling effect on their First Amendment rights. For this reason, it should be undertaken only after thorough consideration and consultation with the institution's legal counsel. If an institution wishes to monitor student online activity for any reason other than suspecting an individual student of wrongdoing, it should work with its legal counsel to establish a policy addressing the the purpose for the monitoring, the conditions under which it will occur, the extent or scope of the monitoring, and what will be done with the resulting information. How each institution addresses this issue will likely vary dramatically by age of the student. For younger students, where some monitoring may make sense for the purpose of protecting the student and teaching him or her how to behave responsibly and safely in the online context, educational institutions will likely be advised to seek parental permission. For older students, particularly adults, general monitoring of online activity is highly questionable. Chapter 6.

May an educational institution search the records of a particular student's online activities if there is a reason to believe the student has been engaged in wrongdoing?

In such a situation, a differentiation must be made between searching devices belonging to the educational institution and those belonging to the student.

The institution should establish whether a student has a reasonable expectation of privacy in the information he or she enters or uses on institutional equipment. This is done by clarifying in the educational institution policies whether students may use institutional devices for personal reasons (and thus have a reasonable expectation of privacy) or not (which would clarify that the student has no reasonable expectation of privacy). If the student has no expectation of privacy in the institutional equipment he or she uses, the educational institution may be justified in searching the contents of that equipment. However, it should also take into consideration the potential chilling effect of doing so. Thus, administration should work with legal counsel in creating a policy addressing such searches that is appropriate for the institution.

If the student does or may have a reasonable expectation of privacy in his or her online activities on the institution's equipment, the institution must be able to meet the *T.L.O.* reasonableness standards before conducting a search: The search must be justified at its inception, which means that the institution must have reasonable grounds for suspecting that the search will disclose evidence of the student's violation of law or institutional policy. It must also be reasonable in scope, meaning that the search should not be any more invasive than necessary to achieve that purpose of discovering that evidence. Note that limiting the scope of a search of electronic devices can be difficult.

In the case of personal electronic devices belonging to students, the law is unsettled, and this is an area of growing debate. For that reason, institutions should discuss this issue with their legal counsel and put in place a policy addressing such situations. Chapter 6.

May an educational institution regulate online activities engaged in by a student outside of the institution, or punish a student for such activities?

Only if the activities constitute a true and serious threat to the educational environment or are intended to reach into the educational environment and are so egregious that they pose a serious risk to safety or otherwise substantially disrupt the educational environment. Chapter 6.

May an educational institution inform parents or other community members of the identity of a student with a communicable disease?

Because educational records are subject to the Family Educational Rights and Privacy Act, personally identifying information may be disclosed without consent if it will help to protect against an imminent danger to the educational community. In such a case, the release must be narrowly tailored to meet the needs of the situation, including the immediacy, magnitude, and specificity of the information released, in the context of the danger presented. The institution must keep detailed records about the release, subject to specific requirements of FERPA. Chapters 2 and 5.

To whom may an official disclose the identity of a student it fears may harm himself/herself or others?

Because educational records are subject to the Family Educational Rights and Privacy Act, personally identifying information may be disclosed without consent if it will help to protect against an imminent danger to the educational community. In such a case, the release must be narrowly tailored to meet the needs of the situation, including the immediacy, magnitude, and specificity of the information released, in the context of the danger presented. The institution must keep detailed records about the release, subject to specific requirements of FERPA. Chapters 2 and 5.

What information may or must an educational institution disclose to parents about students of minority age?

An institution regulated by the Family Educational Rights and Privacy Act (which includes many private institutions) must allow parents of a minority-aged student to inspect the student's current and past "educational records," defined by FERPA as "information directly related to a student" that is maintained by the institution. Various exceptions exist, however; see Chapter 2 for more information. Chapters 2 and 5.

What information may or must an educational institution disclose to parents of adult students?

An institution regulated by the Family Educational Rights and Privacy Act (which includes many private institutions) may not release "educational records" or personally identifiable information about adult students to the student's parents without the student's permission. Some exceptions exist, however; see Chapter 2 for more information. Chapters 2 and 5.

When must a school library or academic library release library records about students?

Release of library records is subject to a variety of laws. A library must comply with court orders, including those issued by FISA under the USA PATRIOT Act. Many library records will be subject to FERPA. Most states have their own laws exempting library records from open records requests, and some state laws go further in protecting the privacy of library records. Furthermore, situations may arise in which these laws contradict each other. For all of these reasons, school and academic libraries should work closely with their institution's legal counsel to establish policy, procedure, and training regarding maintaining library records related to individual students. Chapters 2 and 5.

Does my employer have the right to search my personal belongings when I am in the workplace?

Employees of public institutions are protected by the Fourth Amendment, but many employee rights are also defined by state law. To completely answer this question, you will need to know the law of your own state. In applying the Fourth Amendment to such situations, a court will consider whether a search is "reasonable" in light of the circumstances; the nature and degree of the intrusion on the employee's privacy must be balanced against the governmental interest the employer is attempting to protect. Thus, for example, an employer's actions might be considered reasonable when searching for a work-related file in an employee's filing cabinet, but not searching for the file in the employee's private bags. Chapter 7 and 9.

Does my employer have the right to monitor my phone calls and emails conducted in the workplace?

Employees of public institutions are protected by the Fourth Amendment, but many employee rights are also defined by state law. For example, a few states have recently begun to enact laws specifically protecting the privacy of employee's online activities. So to completely answer this question, you will need to know the law of your own state.

Specifically regarding telephone calls, state laws take different approaches to defining "consent" for the call to be monitored. In some states, only one party to the conversation need know that the call is being monitored for "consent" to be deemed given, even if the other party has no knowledge at all and would object to the monitoring. Monitoring of workplace email likewise may be governed by state law.

In addition, when institutional policies state that an employee's phone calls, email, or other communications may be monitored, the employee will be deemed to have consented to the monitoring. The corollary of this is that if institutional policy states that only work-related communications will be monitored, the employee should have a reasonable expectation of privacy in personal communications (but query the degree to which the employer may be able to separate the two without intercepting some personal communications). Chapter 7.

Can my employer require that I be drug tested? Can I be fired for using drugs outside of the work environment?

If no state law addresses the issue, an educational institution will likely be allowed to require drug testing of employees whose duties directly relate to the safety of students (for example, drug testing is mandated for school bus drivers) or when a reasonable suspicion of drug use by a specific employee exists. However, for an employee of an educational institution to be disciplined based on drug use, factors other than use or possession alone usually are required, such as the use affecting one's job performance. Note that if the institution's policies address drug testing, the employee will be deemed to have consented to the testing as described in the policy. Chapter 7.

Can I be disciplined for my behavior on my own time, including what I post to my personal social media accounts?

State law may address this issue in the brick-and-mortar world, and an increasing number of states are passing laws addressing this question in the on-line world. Beyond specific state law, however, as a general rule, Fourth Amendment protections will allow an educational institution to discipline an employee based on his behavior outside of the workplace only if the behavior seriously and adversely affects the employee's ability to perform his or her job, or otherwise negatively affects the ability of the institution to function well. Chapter 7.

Glossary

anonymize—To remove personally identifying information from a set of data with the assumption that the remaining data can then be used without identifying the individual. Also referred to as *de-identify*.

choice—Principle that individuals should be able to choose whether and what types of information about them is collected and how it is used. See *opt-in, opt-out*.

cloud computing—Using equipment under the ownership and control of a third party to process and/or store information. Examples include Yahoo Mail for email; Google Documents for word processing, spreadsheets, and other documents; Instagram to share photographs; and anything posted on Facebook.

data—Distinct, individual pieces of information.

de-identify—See *anonymize*.

educational records—Under FERPA, any document that contains information that is (1) directly related to a student and (2) maintained by an educational agency or institution, or by a party acting for the agency or institution.

fair information practices—A statement of principles first articulated in the 1970s that, in various forms, has become the basis for much law and regulation limiting the collection and use of personally identifying information.

Federal Trade Commission (FTC)—Oversees the administration of much U.S. law and regulation regarding privacy rights, including the Children's Online Privacy Protection Act.

Fourth Amendment—Refers to constitutional right for individuals to be safe from "unreasonable" searches or seizures by the government or government officials of one's person or possessions. See also *reasonable expectation of privacy, reasonableness, search and seizure*.

FTC—See *Federal Trade Commission*.

generalized search—A search of a group of people based on the suspicion or concern that someone within the group who cannot be specifically identified has engaged in unauthorized activities. Compare to *individualized search*.

individualized search—A search that is directed at an individual due to suspicion based on that individual's behavior. Compare to *generalized search*.

national security letter—Letters used by federal government agencies to compel the provision of information to federal investigators and which, unlike subpoenas, do not require authorization from a judge and are subject to minimal judicial oversight. Compare *subpoena*.

opt-in—The mechanism by which, when personally identifying information is about to be collected, an individual must first specifically indicate which types of PII about him or her may be collected and/or how it may be used; the default is that no PII will be collected and/or used unless and until the subject grants permission. Compare *opt-out*.

opt-out—The mechanism by which, when personally identifying information is about to be collected, an individual may avoid having certain types of PII collected or certain uses of his or her PII being made only by specifically indicating that; the default, without any action on the subject's part, is that all PII will be collected and useable in whatever manner the collector chooses. Compare *opt-in*.

personally identifying (or identifiable) information (PII)—Information that can be used to identify an individual, such as name, address, or Social Security number.

PII—See *personally identifiable information*.

plain view doctrine—Legal doctrine holding that a person cannot have a reasonable expectation of privacy in regard to items clearly visible to others.

reasonable expectation of privacy—Standard used to determine whether the Fourth Amendment applies to a given situation; for the Fourth Amendment to be applicable to a search or seizure, one's expectation of privacy must be reasonable, based on the totality of the circumstances, including one's own behavior and society's expectations under the circumstances. See also *Fourth Amendment, reasonableness, search and seizure*.

reasonableness—A term of art used in analyzing whether one's Fourth Amendment right to be safe from "unreasonable" searches and seizures has been violated. When conducted by educational officials (but not law enforcement officers), a search or seizure is reasonable if it is justified at its inception and reasonably related in scope to the circumstances that justified the search, based on all the factors of the situation. See Chapter 5.

right of publicity—A matter of state law; specific definitions and laws will differ. Usually refers to one's right to control the use of one's "likeness" (pictures, name, voice, or other representations that are associated with the individual) in a commercial manner.

search and seizure—Generally refers to the Fourth Amendment constitutional right to not be subject to "unreasonable" searches or seizures by the government or government officials of one's person or possessions. See also *Fourth Amendment, reasonable expectation of privacy, reasonableness*.

seizure—For Fourth Amendment purposes, a seizure occurs when a person is detained under conditions in which a reasonable person would have believed that he or she was not free to leave.

subpoena—a court order requiring a witness to appear in court at a particular time and place to testify and/or produce documents.

tort—A private or civil wrong or injury done to an individual in violation of law for which a legal remedy is available in the form of monetary damages.

Resources for Further Research

The following resources are only a few of many excellent resources available on the plethora of privacy topics relevant in the educational environment. As always, as you make use of these resources, think critically about the source, and in particular check for dates and currency of information.

GENERAL

Print

Adams, Helen R., Robert F. Bocher, Carol A. Gordon, and Elizabeth Barry-Kessler, *Privacy in the 21st Century: Issues for Public, School, and Academic Libraries* (Westport, CT: Libraries Unlimited, 2005).

Alexander, Kern, and M. David Alexander, *The Law of Schools, Students and Teachers in a Nutshell* (St. Paul, MN: West Publishing Co., 2003).

Andrews, Lori, *I Know Who You Are and I Saw What You Did: Social Networks and the Death of Privacy* (New York: Free Press, 2011).

Chmara, Theresa, *Privacy and Confidentiality Issues: A Guide for Libraries and Their Lawyers* (Chicago: American Library Association, 2009).

Essex, Nathan L., *School Law and the Public Schools: A Practical Guide for Educational Leaders*, 5th ed. (Upper Saddle River, NJ: Pearson Education, Inc., 2012).

Kaplin, William A., and Barbara A. Lee, *The Law of Higher Education* (Washington, D.C.: National Association of College and University Attorneys, 2007).

Minow, Mary, and Tomas A. Lipinski, *The Library's Legal Answer Book* (Chicago: American Library Association, 2003).

Solove, Daniel J., *Understanding Privacy* (Cambridge, MA: Harvard University Press, 2010).

Solove, Daniel J., and Paul M. Schwartz, *Privacy, Information, and Technology*, 3rd ed. (New York: Wolters Kluwer Law & Business, 2011).

Warnick, Bryan R., *Understanding Student Rights in Schools: Speech, Religion, and Privacy in Educational Settings* (New York: Teachers College Press, Teachers College, Columbia University, 2013).

Online

American Civil Liberties Union (ACLU)
www.aclu.org
> The ACLU website provides a wealth of information on a wide range of civil liberties, including privacy and First Amendment issues, and thus is a good resource for the interaction of these issues that incorporate different legal areas. The site has a specific grouping of issues labeled "Protecting Civil Liberties in the Digital Age."

American Library Association, "Privacy Tool Kit"
www.ala.org/offices/oif/iftoolkits/toolkitsprivacy/default
> Although the primary target is librarians, this website is valuable for educators at all levels in understanding privacy and its relationship to information access. It also provides action tools that can be adapted for use within your specific community.

Center for Democracy & Technology (CDT)
www.cdt.org
> The CDT describes itself as "the leading Internet freedom organization working at the critical edge of policy innovation." The website provides current and thorough information on a variety of issues related to information on the Internet and the safety of Internet users, including privacy and freedom of expression.

Education Law Association
www.educationlaw.org
> The Education Law Association is a national, nonprofit member association offering information about current legal issues affecting education and the rights of those involved in education in both public and private K–12 schools, universities, and colleges.

Electronic Frontier Foundation (EFF)
www.eff.org
> The EFF is an activist and advocacy organization that has been paramount throughout its history in protecting the rights of Internet users. The website offers information on current issues, debates, pending legislation, and pending court cases in the areas of privacy, free speech, copyright fair use, and more.

Electronic Privacy Information Center (EPIC)
www.epic.org
> EPIC provides background information on a wide variety of privacy issues as well as serving as a very thorough current update resource, so I have not

listed the pertinent subsections in this Resource List. Rather, I encourage you to peruse the list of issues in the left menu of the website. Issues include cloud computing, children's online privacy, cybersecurity, Facebook, locational privacy, search engine privacy, social networking privacy, and student privacy.

Privacy International
www.privacyinternational.org
  Privacy International's mission is to defend the right to privacy across the world, and to fight unlawful surveillance and other intrusions into private life by governments and corporations. The website provides information regarding privacy in a wide variety of settings at an international level, including data protection, communications surveillance, consumer protection, and identity cards.

Privacy Rights Clearinghouse (PRC)
www.privacyrights.org
  The PRC's primary goals include raising individual awareness of how technology affects privacy, empowering individuals to take action to control what happens with their own personal information, and advocating for information users' rights. The website provides information on privacy in contexts that include education and online privacy.

ABOUT FEDERAL PRIVACY LAWS

Center for Democracy & Technology, "ECPA"
www.cdt.org/category/blogtags/ecpa

Daggett, Lynn M., "Student Privacy and the Protection of Pupil Rights Act as Amended by No Child Left Behind," 12 *U.C. Davis J. of Juvenile L. & Pol'y* 51 (2008)
jjlp.law.ucdavis.edu/archives/vol-12-no-1/Daggett.pdf

Digital Due Process, "ECPA Reform"
www.digitaldueprocess.org/index.cfm?objectid=37940370-2551-11DF-8E020 00C296BA163

Electronic Privacy Information Center, "National Security Letters"
epic.org/privacy/nsl/

Electronic Privacy Information Center, "USA Patriot Act"
epic.org/privacy/terrorism/usapatriot/

Federal Trade Commission, "COPPA FAQs"
www.ftc.gov/privacy/coppafaqs.shtm

U.S. Department of Education, "Family Educational Rights and Privacy Act (FERPA)"
www2.ed.gov/policy/gen/guid/fpco/ferpa/index.html

U.S. Department of Education, "Family Educational Rights and Privacy Act (FERPA) and the Disclosure of Student Information Related to Emergencies and Disasters"
www2.ed.gov/policy/gen/guid/fpco/pdf/ferpa-disaster-guidance.pdf

SPECIFIC ISSUES

American Civil Liberties Union, "Protecting Civil Liberties in the Digital Age: Students"
www.aclu.org/technology-and-liberty/students

American Civil Liberties Union, "Workplace Privacy"
www.aclu.org/technology-and-liberty/workplace-privacy

American Library Association, "State Privacy Laws Regarding Library Records"
www.ala.org/offices/oif/ifgroups/stateifcchairs/stateifcinaction/stateprivacy

Cyberbullying Research Center
www.cyberbullying.us/

First Amendment Center, "First Amendment Schools"
www.firstamendmentschools.org/

International Association of Privacy Professionals, "Best Practices in Drafting Plain-Language and Layered Privacy Policies"
www.privacyassociation.org/publications/2012_09_13_best_practices_in_drafting_plain_language_and_layered_privacy

Minor, Maria, Henry M. Brashen, and Gina Smith, "Cyber Bullying in Higher Education,"
www.waldenu.edu/~/media/Files/WAL/about/cyber-bullying-in-higher-education.ashx

OnGuardOnline.gov, "Kids' Privacy"
www.onguardonline.gov/articles/0031-kids-privacy

Privacy Rights Clearinghouse, "Privacy in Education: Guide for Parents and Adult-Age Students"
www.privacyrights.org/fs/fs29-education.htm

Privacy Rights Clearinghouse, "Workplace Privacy and Employee Monitoring"
www.privacyrights.org/fs/fs7-work.htm

Child Welfare Information Gateway, "How to Report Suspected Child Maltreatment"
www.childwelfare.gov/responding/how.cfm

Shmoop, "Right to Privacy"
www.shmoop.com/right-to-privacy/

Surveillance Self-Defense, "Warrantless Searches"
ssd.eff.org/your-computer/govt/warrantless

Index

About the Author

GRETCHEN McCORD, MSIS, JD, is an attorney-consultant and trainer in the areas of copyright and privacy law. A licensed attorney since 2001, Gretchen practiced as an academic librarian for years before beginning law school. She practiced copyright, privacy, and trademark law in major law firms for over eight years before establishing her own practice as an attorney-consultant and educator in the areas of copyright and privacy law. In addition to providing legal services, she conducts a variety of training, from face-to-face workshops to webinars, in these areas, specializing in assisting educational institutions, libraries, and non-profit organizations in transitioning into the digital world.

Gretchen has served in library and community leadership roles for over 20 years, including as president of the Texas Library Association, member of the City of Austin Library Commission, chair of the Friends of the Libraries and Archives of Texas, and chair of Groups United to Advocate Responsible Development. She writes and speaks extensively on copyright and privacy issues, and related issues and is the author of *Copyright in Cyberspace: Questions and Answers for Librarians*.

You can contact and follow Gretchen at any or all of the following:

Gretchen@digitalinfolaw.com

www.digitalinfolaw.com

facebook.com/digital.information.law

Twitter:@GMcCordLaw

linkedin.com/in/gretchenmccord

3M

CPSIA information can be obtained at www.ICGtesting.com
Printed in the USA
LVOW02s0431030414

380123LV00006B/37/P

9 781610 690812